JUMPSHIP

JOSH SHIPP

JUMPSHIP

Ditch Your Dead-End Job
and Turn Your Passion
into a Profession

ST. MARTIN'S PRESS

NEW YORK

www.stmartins.com

Library of Congress Cataloging-in-Publication Data

Shipp, Josh.
    Jump ship : ditch your dead-end job and turn your passion into a profession /
Josh Shipp.—First U.S. edition.
        pp. cm.
    Includes bibliographical references.
    ISBN 978-0-312-64673-8 (hardcover)
    ISBN 978-1-250-01751-2 (e-book)
    1. Career changes.   2. Career development.   I. Title.
    HF5384.S553 2013
    650.14—dc23

                                                    2013023832

St. Martin's Press books may be purchased for educational, business, or promotional use. For information on bulk purchases, please contact Macmillan Corporate and Premium Sales Department at 1-800-221-7945, extension 5442, or write special markets@macmillan.com.

First Edition: December 2013

10 9 8 7 6 5 4 3 2 1

For Sarah. You make everything seem possible and worthwhile.

CONTENTS

JUMPSHIP

A PROPER INTRODUCTION

Well, hello, I'm Josh Shipp, and you and I don't have much in common.

I know it's a bit unconventional for an author to potentially alienate his readers right out of the gate, but I'm not particularly conventional. As you'll discover, that's just not me, and it's not really what matters anyway. Fact is, this isn't your typical be-your-own-boss, make-a-gazillion-dollars-and-be-superhappy-all-the-time-without-having-to-work-hard book, filled with feel-good lies and fantasies. I'm not writing this to tell you all the things you want to hear; I'm writing this to tell you what you *need* to hear if you're really serious about making a career change and truly succeeding.

I have a reputation for being "in your face, but on your side," and I make it a habit to shoot straight with people, period. Which is why I feel obligated to open this book by addressing our differences head-on.

Some of those differences, you'll likely agree, are good things. For example, you probably were not abandoned by your birth parents and raised in the foster care system. You probably weren't written off as a lost cause when you were a child; probably weren't obese, abused, and suicidal in junior high. You probably never spent a night in jail in high school. Furthermore, the gentlemen among you probably grew past 5′ 7″ and could sport facial hair if you so pleased. I, however, am often mistaken for a man-boy.

But there's at least one way we're different that you're perhaps jealous of: I'm living my dream . . . and you're probably not.

Wow, Josh, seriously?! This book is the worst, and I hate you. Sorry. But I didn't say that to crush your spirits. It's simply the truth: I'm living my dream. And it's a truth that I wish for you as well.

Let's face the facts here: You're reading a book about how to change careers and find your dream job. I'm guessing you know deep down that you are capable of something much more than what you're doing right now. I'm betting you look around at your life sometimes and think: "This can't possibly be all there is!" If that's where you're at, then I'm delighted you found this book. Before we're done here, the path from Where You Are to Where You Want to Be will be clear. But it will be on you to implement said clear path.

Oddly, I've never wanted to quit my job. Seriously. I started doing what I love when I was still in high school and have never looked back. I got my start as a professional speaker when I was seventeen, and I continue to speak at high schools and colleges worldwide. I host and produce documentary television shows. I train other speakers who want to reach youth audiences. And, obviously, I write books.

I'm married to an incredible Italian woman named Sarah, who gave me two children, London and Katie. London, much to his good fortune, looks a lot like Sarah. He speaks Italian and has stunning olive skin and an enormous heart. Katie, on the other hand, takes after me. She's small and pasty and spends the majority of her time crying. The difference is that the pediatricians say she'll grow out of that since she's a baby, while they offered me no similar encouragement. I'm happy for her, and have accepted myself.

Also, in the interest of full disclosure, I just turned thirty, which makes me feel old, so I've taken to wearing cardigans and having an afternoon nap. But I'm still active. I like to run. I eat healthfully. I juice. And we live in what I consider to be the happiest place on the planet: California.

Maybe all this doesn't sound like your dream at all—your dream is bound to look different than mine, as it should. But I'm living the life I've always wanted, and there's seriously no good reason why you shouldn't do the same.

Now, some of you clever overachiever types are starting to wonder why a guy like me, who's never changed careers—and never even *wanted* to—decided to write a book about jumping ship. Your arms are crossed, your brow is furrowed, and you're asking yourself: "Could anyone be less qualified to talk about this?"

I decided to write this book because somewhere around my midtwenties, I realized I wasn't normal. Most people's stories are more like yours; somewhere around their midtwenties, they begin to suspect they're on the wrong track—and they want off. Stat.

I've seen countless friends, peers, and fellow millennials go through what you're going through—the boredom, the frustration, the hidden shame, the confusion, and the paralysis of coming to grips with the fact that they don't like where they are, what they're doing, and where they're going. I've walked step-by-step through this transition with many of them. Through all this, I started thinking a lot about what I'd done differently—how I'd ended up in such a different place than so many of my peers.

This book is the result. Through a lot of self-reflection, I was able to reverse engineer my success story. Then things got even better. As I began to have conversations with brave people in my life who've had the guts to chuck the script other people were writing for their lives and Jump Ship to pursue their dreams, I realized I wasn't just a fluke. These brave people had all followed the same steps I had. Some started young, like I did, and others changed course somewhere along the line. In both cases, the steps we all followed to success looked remarkably similar. And so I set pen to paper to record the patented Seven-Step Blueprint for Dream-Job Fulfillment (patent pending).

Later in this book we'll get into the nitty-gritty of the seven-step process for landing your dream job, but I want to take a second up front to emphasize that this isn't just some schtick. When I sat down to map this out, I didn't know if it would be three steps or ten steps. It turned out to be seven. And these steps have come through years and years of personal experience and the stories that come from many of my successful friends. Seven isn't a magic number. The number of steps isn't the point, or ultimately that important. What's important is that the principles can be applied to your story and the stories of the people around you, and that they work.

You've probably heard the phrase "jump ship" before, right? I've used it already in this introduction. It's slang for "bailing out," which is similar to the phrase "turning tail," or—to use a now-antiquated cultural jest—"taking French leave," all of which are slang for quitting, fleeing, escaping, or abandoning the course you're on. At its most basic level, this book is about that concept.

I want to help you escape—or even avoid, should you be so lucky—the increasingly common quarter-life crisis by giving you the kick in the pants you need to make a "jump" away from your current career path to one that makes your heart come alive. I want to help you recapture that carefree enthusiasm you might not have felt since you were a kid, back when you jumped out of trees and sprinted down hills and did flips off monkey bars without even considering that you might break an ankle.

This book wants you to identify *that* job—the dream job you want for the rest of your life—and then help you get there.

Remember all those differences between us that we were talking about earlier? I want you to set those aside for a second and hear me loud and clear: We're also very similar. I'm an imperfect human just like you. I was born with no particular advantage—no wealth, no connections. My parents left me with a name and nothing else. Not even particularly hardy genes.

If, for one second, you place me on a pedestal as if I'm on a higher level than you because I've "made it" and you haven't (yet), you're completely offtrack and you're going to miss the whole point.

Remember the old *Saturday Night Live* skit where Will Ferrell is the cowbell player in Blue Öyster Cult as they record "Don't Fear the Reaper"? If not, do a quick Google search to find and watch it. It's an *SNL* classic.

As great as Will Ferrell is, I must say my favorite character in the skit is Christopher Walken playing Bruce Dickinson, a famous producer who, in the skit, comes in every now and then to comment on the usage of the cowbell, making instantly famous such lines such as, "Guess what . . . I gotta fever, and the only prescription is more cowbell!" But my favorite moment is when he says:

I put on my pants just like the rest of you—one leg at a time. Except, once my pants are on, I make gold records.

I want to be like Bruce Dickinson. I want to wake up every day, put on my pants, *and then go make gold records.*

And that's exactly what I set out to do every day in my life. I don't say that to impress you, but to impress upon you that *anything* I have done with my life—any success, speaking engagement, TV show, interview, book contract, new business, or partnership—all happened because I (after securing my pants) put the blood, sweat, and tears into making those goals a reality.

I didn't write this book because I'm better than you or have everything figured out. I'm a massive, chronic screwup, and I'm still on a journey of my own. I wrote this because I've learned a lot (usually the hard way) as I've pursued my dreams, and I would love nothing more than to share those lessons with you.

Of course, I put my pants on one leg at a time, just like you and everyone else. But what I choose to do next is what separates me from the millions of people who set their dream aside on an attic shelf—next to their high school varsity jackets, yearbooks, and dusty trophies—and accidentally forget about it. And, this is important: What YOU do next will determine if you are one of them or one of us.

The lessons I share in these pages involve some of the most important decisions I've ever made. I honestly believe the ideas in this book could change the course of your entire life.

If you think I'm talking about a simple career change here, I'm not. This is bigger than just your career. It's about finding what you really want to do with your life, dealing with what's holding you back, and actually going for it. This is a little thing that will change everything—your life and the lives of those you influence.

One of my favorite quotes is by Maya Angelou. And, I admit, after being alive on this planet for over three decades filled with both amazing and painful memories, I can wholeheartedly agree with her when she says:

> *There is no greater agony than bearing an untold story inside you.*

Does reading that make your heart hurt a tad? I know it does mine because I am still, with everything that I am, continuing on the journey of telling my story. In fact, writing this book is part of that story for me, and I hope reading it can become part of your story. If that quote makes your gut turn over, you probably have passions, desires, and hopes similar to mine. You probably also have sleepless nights with panicky feelings as you realize your life is passing and you haven't done the one thing you know above all else that you were put on this planet to do. If you are that person and you are daily experiencing the agony of the story that has gone untold in your life, then I should let you know, "*You've gotta fever and the only prescription is for you to Jump Ship . . .*"

You spend a third of your life sleeping and a third of your life working. If that working third of your life is messed up, the ways you spend time with the people you love will be messed up as well.

Finding that dream job and living in that sweet spot can give you the purpose to get out of bed. It can save your marriage or potentially stop a bad one from happening. It can turn you into a positive role model for your (future?) children. The benefits are virtually endless. But, if you ever want to find your right thing, you've gotta quit that wrong thing.

Tomorrow, you are going to wake up and you are going to put on a pair of pants. The real question I have for you is: What are you going to do postpants?

I'll be making gold records, and I'd love for you to join me.

—JOSH SHIPP

PS: If this is going to be a proper "introduction," I'd like to get to know you a bit as well.

Please send me a tweet at @JoshShipp and let me know what career you are in now and what your dream gig is.

Pleasure to make your acquaintance, fellow traveler. Let's get this journey started . . .

PART ONE: Before the Jump

It's Time for a Change

> *Most of us have two lives. The life we live, and the unlived life within us. Between the two stands Resistance.*
>
> —STEVEN PRESSFIELD

If you're reading this, I'm going to make an assumption about you: Life is not how you thought it would be.

This probably won't come as a surprise, but your experience is actually pretty common, especially among people our age (the not-so-recent graduates, twentysomethings, and young professionals of the world). There's even a sociological term for it: quarter-life crisis. That's right—you don't have to wait until midlife to have a crisis of your own anymore. And, unlike in the crises of midlife, you probably don't have nearly enough money just yet to distract yourself with a shiny new sports car, plastic surgery, or a set of golf clubs.

The quarter-life crisis—characterized by insecurities, disappointments, loneliness, and depression—typically strikes twenty- and thirtysomethings shortly after they enter the "real world." In fact, a recent study by the Depression Alliance (like the Avengers, only really sad) found that a third of all people in their twenties feel depressed.

Why? All sorts of reasons, but it all boils down to a feeling that your life is on the wrong track. You're drifting toward a distant shore you have no desire to reach while your real dreams fade further and further into the unreachable distance.

Which is confusing and, honestly, just doesn't seem fair. You really aren't asking for much: You just want a job that combines your passions and skills, provides a reasonable income, and allows you to spend time with people you love. And the dead-end, soul-deadening job you've been clocking into for the last few years isn't exactly all you'd hoped and dreamed for yourself. Work isn't your life, you say, yet (like it or not) it takes up a pretty big chunk of it—about 33 percent big. So . . . why are you spending a third of your life doing something you never wanted to?

You've barely lived three decades and you're already wracked with regrets.

Maybe you don't even hate the work itself. You may even like your boss and consider many of your colleagues your friends. What you hate is that forty, fifty, sixty hours of your week don't feel anything like the few hours you get every now and again when you find time to do the thing you really love. You hate that you have to lay your dreams aside every Monday morning.

Still, you probably have your reasons for staying in that job that's making you miserable: You need a steady paycheck and health insurance, or you'd rather tough it out in a bad situation you're familiar with than risk something new. I get it. But here's my advice for you:

QUIT.

You can quit, you know. It's okay. Forget what you've heard about winners never quitting, because that's just not true. Smart people quit the right things at the right time. And, let's be hon-

est, how's the whole "sticking it out" approach working for you?
Do you feel like a winner right now? Or completely defeated?

Here are three all-too-common signs that it's high time to call
it quits and move on:

You're unsatisfied

Don't worry, you're not alone—most surveys over the last
three years agree that less than 40 percent of Americans are
satisfied with their work. Generally, the numbers are even
worse for those under the age of twenty-five, where we're
posting the lowest job satisfaction rates since 1987. In other
cheery news, worker unhappiness has shown a consistent
upward trend in that time. Now, maybe you're unhappy
because you're just a grouchy person; but I believe most
people are unhappy because they're just not doing what
they know they should be.

You're bored

Another prime indicator is boredom. A report from the
Conference Board found only half the U.S. workforce even
finds their job interesting. To me, that's shocking and sad.
But let's face it: A lot of boring stuff happens at most
companies, which means you're probably asked to work on
a lot of it. The fact that the work is relatively easy or that it
pays a lot doesn't really compensate after a while, and you
start to feel like you're wasting your time. If your work
doesn't challenge you or make good use of your strengths,
I think it's time to go.

You're stuck

As many as a third of all American workers feel like their
careers have reached a dead end. You could even be content

with your pay grade and indifferent to "climbing the corporate ladder" and still feel like there's no room for you to grow. If you've learned everything you can, contributed everything you have to contribute, and continue to clock in only because you don't know what else to do or where to go, start planning your exit.

There are a thousand other subtle signs it's time for a change, but one of them in particular is my favorite and, really, the heartbeat behind this book.

One of the best reasons to change directions—to Jump Ship, so to speak—is because you know there's something you actually care about.

If you're more excited about your hobby than you are about your job, look for a job related to your hobby. If you have a gift or a skill that makes your heart sing like Taylor Swift every time you use it, get paid for using that gift. If you've always dreamed of owning an animal shelter or working as a Hollywood makeup artist—and you've got the talent for these things—drop what you're doing and start pursuing it now. It's going to take a while to earn success, so why not start earning it now?

Walking into work on Monday and wishing you were "anywhere else" is one thing. Ordinary discontent, maybe. But walking into work on Monday and wishing you were writing, speaking, cooking, gardening, decorating, designing, strategizing, building, investing, or teaching—some specific desire that wells up inside you and pulls at the corners of your mind—is something else entirely. That is a dream longing to be lived.

I Believe That You Were Born with a Purpose

You were created to make something of your life that no other person on the planet or in the history of the world ever could. If you don't do it, it might never be done. And you, and only you, know what that thing is. This is your dream, and if you don't bring your dream to life, your dream dies with you.

I dare you to deny that it's true. Deep in your heart, you know that this thing—this dream—lives within you. And you have to pursue it. You have to at least try. The fact that you haven't tried is, I believe, why you're so bummed out and discouraged about your life right now. The life you were born to live remains un-lived within you.

It's important that you hear this: It's not too late to pursue your dream. And, nine times out of ten, it's probably possible to get paid for it, too. I'm not saying you'll get rich (although you may). But having the whole world means nothing if you gain it at the expense of your soul.

I know that sounds serious, but that's because I take all this pretty seriously. I've seen what a difference it can make in a person's life when they're working a job that makes them come alive. Many of my friends and peers have made the jump. I've helped dozens of people like you make the jump and docu-mented the process to encourage others to do the same.

So many people in your shoes do nothing. Remember how I said earlier that fewer than 40 percent of Americans report feel-ing satisfied with their jobs? Another study done in early 2012 by Accenture found that 70 percent of unhappy employees *planned to stay put*. If you're a normal human being, raised with school counselors telling you exactly what grades would get you which scholarships and which college programs would get you which careers, you probably have trouble cutting through all the stuff programmed into you. You might not feel like you have permis-sion to just abandon the norm, Jump Ship, and go after your dreams.

After all, according to tradition and honor . . .

Captains Go Down with Their Ships

Or so the saying goes. Turns out that there's actually a lot of legend and misinformation surrounding the whole idea. And, for the sake of this metaphor, there are a few other things we ought to clarify.

There was an embarrassing and rather tragic incident in January 2012 where the *Costa Concordia,* a 4,200 passenger Italian cruise ship, ran aground off the coast of Italy when a combination of "human error" and "violations" of the company's safety guidelines brought the vessel too close to shore. Basically, the captain was an idiot. To make matters worse, he was one of the first persons to abandon ship, leaving the crew and passengers behind in chaos. He later claimed that he had "left the ship accidentally" after tripping and falling into a rescue craft. Poor man. From his story, I suspect he has a long history of similar misfortunes; I wouldn't be at all surprised to learn that, as a child, his dog often ate his homework.

Following this incident, however, there was a sudden interest in the old phrase "a captain goes down with his ship," where it comes from and whether it has any basis in law.

It's a noble concept. It is thought that the whole idea derives from the medieval ideal of chivalry, which (to oversimplify) basically teaches that people of high station or power have the moral obligation to look after those who are disadvantaged. Anyway, there are a bunch of stories from the late nineteenth and early twentieth centuries of captains who, when their vessels were in distress, put themselves in danger to evacuate the passengers and personnel. Captain Smith of the doomed RMS *Titanic* is probably the captain who most people associate with this expression, although the idea predates him (and there's some debate about the good captain's actual conduct as the ship went down). There is also a rather famous story about a Japanese admiral in World War II who insisted on going down with his sinking aircraft carrier rather than be rescued.

The principle is clear: The captain will be the last person to leave the ship alive prior to its sinking or destruction, and, if unable to rescue his crew and passengers, the captain will not evacuate himself.

The idea sounds noble—and it is. But in the context of your work and your dreams, your personal moral obligation is most certainly *not* to go down with the ship. In fact, it is one of the most compelling reasons *to* make the jump.

Why do I say this? Two reasons: (1) each and every one of you is a captain; (2) none of you is on your own ship.

This ship you're on, this job you work for, this company you work for, isn't *your* ship. Whether or not it goes down at sea is not your concern or responsibility. You're just a passenger.

You see, no one has ever suggested a captain go down with just any old ship, like it's their duty as captains to climb aboard the first doomed vessel they see and proudly drown. No one calls that fool a hero. Captains are expected to go down with *their* ship. Ultimately, this phrase is about taking personal responsibility for those under your care, not about staying needlessly in a hopeless situation. It's about doing everything you can—even if it costs you your life—to protect and save what has been entrusted to you. But sometimes you're just a passenger on someone else's ship, and from where you sit, it doesn't look good. Or the captain is steering in a direction you never wanted to go. Or you're under attack from pirates. Get out. Save yourself.

But really, when I'm telling you to Jump Ship, I'm not simply encouraging you to save yourself. This isn't a book about how to be a selfish brat that doesn't give a rip about the thousands of

16 JUMP SHIP

people drowning around you. In fact, by the end of all this, you'll
be in excellent condition to pull all kinds of people out of the
ocean. It's just that, right now, you have a bigger concern.

Your Ship Is in Trouble
It might be a perfectly sound vessel on a straight course. But it's
going to someplace you just don't want to go. It's someone else's
ship, and it's working great for them. The problem is that while
you've been taking a ride on someone else's ship, your own vessel
drifts toward a rocky coastline with no one at the helm. The ship
I'm talking about—the ship you should be concerned about—is
the one you were born to command. It's time to get your ship
together. (Forgive me.)

The ship you command is the U.S.S. *One and Only Life.*
Where are you steering her? For that matter, are you steering
at all? Or are you stowing away in third class—given up on your
"one and only life"—and surrendered the tiller to others or let
her drift along wherever the current takes her?

What too many people do is simply leap from sinking ship
to sinking ship, looking for happiness in other people's dreams.
They know they're headed the wrong way—they can tell something isn't right—but they just think quitting is the answer.
They need a fresh start, that's all.

The other day I heard someone say that quitting your job is
the new American Dream. I hope it isn't. Quitting all by itself
is a stupid goal and an empty dream. Sometimes the way people
talk about retirement has the same hollow feel—like work is just
this sad, awful thing you have to spend all your life doing until
maybe finally you have enough money to quit and enjoy doing
nothing for a few years before your body stops working. Ugh.
Depressing, right?

I think older generations helped shape these attitudes. Not

that it's your parents' fault that you hate your job. It's a cultural thing. For generations and generations, people have been stewing in their regrets and passing down faulty thinking. How often have you heard someone say to a young person who's preparing to travel internationally or volunteer with a cause they believe in something along the lines of "Enjoy it while you can" or "Get it out of your system while you're young"? As if everything fun is off-limits once you enter the workforce. No more travel to Europe or volunteering overseas or learning new things once you're a grown-up. Grown-ups have to be practical—and apparently unhappy—until they retire and prepare to die. Oh, what fun.

Maybe it's somehow comforting to older people to think that they "couldn't" pursue their dreams once they were older. It makes a great excuse. After all, if they didn't have a choice but to settle down, they can't help it that they didn't live their dream. It's easier to believe—and teach, consciously or not—that idealism is for kids or that living your dream is a childhood fantasy than it is to face the possibility that they abandoned their dreams.

I don't want this strong statement to be seen as speculation. I continually see this sort of thinking again and again.

Don't make the fatal mistake of clinging to beliefs about yourself and your circumstances that simply don't match reality. Hear me: You are not locked in. Your fate isn't sealed. That feeling of being trapped in a downward spiral is an illusion. You can break free, you can find and make a living doing what you love, and I can show you the way.

It's your choice to follow.

If your ship has run aground, if you're off course, as the captain of your life you have to take responsibility for righting the ship and changing direction. Maybe you've been jumping from deck to deck chasing other people's dreams all over the sea for the last ten years; you could be miles from your own ship right now, and it'll be an adventure just to find her, let alone take the wheel. But you're the captain. You have to jump.

I know it's scary. If you had already overcome your fears, you'd already be living your dream. You'd be writing this book, not reading it. But, believe it or not, being scared is another sign that it's time to jump. It's okay to be scared. Change is scary! But think about this: If you stay put and change nothing, where will you be in ten, twenty, fifty years from now? If you suspect you'll wake up in the middle of a midlife crisis wracked with regret, dreaming about what could have been and saying things like, "I wish I'd . . . ," "It's too late," and "If only," do yourself a favor and take the risk. There comes a time when the risks of staying outweigh the risks of going. The fact that you're scared to try it is a pretty good sign that you want it really badly.

You're probably itching to jump, and you're probably wishing I'd hurry up and drop some knowledge on you that will magically reveal everything you need to know. Maybe you're tempted to skip this whole first section and sink your teeth into the seven steps.

I have some unpopular, counterintuitive, and seemingly contradictory advice for you first.

Don't Quit Your Day Job . . . Yet

Honestly, that's probably one of the worst things you can do right now. You may feel ready to Jump Ship, but you're not prepared to. How do I know? If you were, you would have done so already.

Seeing that you haven't, it would seem prudent to take advantage of this moment to prepare for the jump. If you learn to start dreaming the right way and wait to quit at the right time, your day job could even be your ally in this crazy adventure.

What you're considering is extremely difficult. Seven steps might sound simple enough, but look around you for a second and ask yourself how many people you know are actually living their dreams. Jumping isn't normal. It isn't natural. You are on the edge of something extraordinary. And it will be really, really, really, really hard.

So, back away from the rail for a second; we don't want you just throwing yourself overboard and hoping for the best. There will come a time—probably long before you feel "ready"—when you'll have to make the leap. But until you have something to jump for or toward, you're jumping into free fall, and, if you don't unload some baggage first, you'll sink like a rock in the open ocean.

Spoiler alert: Jumping isn't the first step. Dreams take planning, purpose, and progress to succeed.

You've heard it said that "success comes when preparation meets opportunity." The opportunity to quit will always be there. It takes a little more patience to wait for the right time to jump for your dream, and quite a bit of work—some physical, but a lot of it mental—before you're actually prepared to take advantage of the opportunity.

I hate to say this, but . . .

This Book Might NOT Help You

There's a reason I didn't just open this book by diving into the seven steps. The fact of the matter is that these seven steps won't help you at all if we don't address a few core things up front. There's a chance they could just make everything worse and make you even more miserable.

My fear is that you'll read this book and gain some useful info . . . and then do nothing. That would be awful. I mean, either way, my family thanks you for buying the book and all, but, seriously, what a waste! Not only would you still be in the same unhappy situation you were when you started, but on top of that you'd know exactly what you needed to do to change it. You'd be without excuses, and you'd know it. I wouldn't wish that guilt and shame on anyone.

So, I have to ask you (and I will ask you again): Are you serious about this? If you're not willing to quit being a passenger on someone else's boat and claim command of your life, please don't bother reading any further.

I don't have time for people who only want to talk. I've spent far too many wasted hours in conversations, sharing lunches or coffee with people who I can immediately see—almost like my own personal spidey-sense—will *never* have the guts to carry out their grandiose plan. There is nothing more frustrating than watching a person paint a weak and undefined vision for the future, with little to no passion and no defined goals as I nod my head and look straight into their heart, suspecting with incredible accuracy that they don't have the guts to pull it off. These people are more in love with the image in their head than they are with seeing it become a reality in their lives.

So let's cut to the chase. Do you have the guts? If not, go read something else. Save yourself some time. And I mean that honestly. This book is only going to frustrate you even further if you don't have the deep desire to change your own future. You know the phrase "ignorance is bliss"? Well, this is your moment to happily choose your own ignorance.

On the other hand, if you feel you've got the guts to pull this off, if you're tired of all the "easy solutions" on the market and are determined to take risks and put in the work, let's do this.

I want you to jump, I really do. But here's the truth: The only people who jump are the people who want to. The only thing that matters is that *you* want to jump.

If you're willing, if you want to learn how, then read on. It's a long journey, but it's worth it, and I'll help you find the way.

Finding Yourself (Part One)

I hope you're feeling impatient right now. If you are drooling because you feel like I'm dangling the "Seven-Step Dream Job" carrot in front of your face, good—that means you really want it.

But over the next few chapters, I'm going to ask you to hold your horses. Remember, the opportunity to quit your job will always be there; the key to a successful jump lies in the preparation.

So, in the interest of prepping you well, I'm going to lay down some knowledge. These next chapters before we get to the seven steps aren't just irrelevant stories or random rants. These are a few life lessons that I had to learn (most of them the hard way) and that allowed me to be in a place where I was ready to jump—to go for my dreams and not look back.

Remember, I've been working my dream job my whole adult life. This isn't because I was smarter than you. It's because life dealt me a terrible hand and forced me to learn a lot of hard lessons early on. At the time, it was the worst, and I almost didn't make it. But looking back, I realize that, in a strange way, I got lucky.

These principles prepped me to do what I needed to do, and I think they will strengthen your ability to Jump Ship, too. We'll

spend plenty of time going over all the practical step-by-step lessons in Part Two—plus personal stories of successes and failures,
crazy, harebrained theories, and, most likely, quite a bit of rant-
ing and raving about things that may or may not be important to
you. But before we start down the step-by-step path, we have to
lay a foundation.

Think about it: If you don't have solid ground to jump from,
you're not really jumping, are you? You're either stuck in the
mud or floating through space.

This book exists to highlight an opportunity and help you
seize it: the chance to make a career change, to quit something
you don't like in order to pursue something you love. Before you
can do that, however, you need to find yourself.

I Have a Problem

It's hard to convey the seriousness of this problem, since I was
born with it and I've never known life without it. It's dangerous.
It affects my family, my travels, my energy level, and my mood.

At any given moment, whether I'm driving or on foot, whether
I'm in a foreign city or in my own neighborhood, *I have no idea
where I am.*

I'm serious. You know how some people have a natural sense
of direction? Like, they'll squint in the direction of the sun for
a few seconds (even on a cloudy day) and just know which way is
north? I'm the exact opposite of those people. Tell me that something is north and send me off to find it and you'll find me days
later, deranged and dehydrated, wandering off to the southeast.

Actually, it's worse than that. Forget the points on a compass
or reading a map—I even have a hard time following simple directions like "turn right." You know the old trick you teach kids
to help them tell left from right? The one where you hold up
your hands in front of you and extend your thumb and forefin-

ger and the hand that forms an L is left and the other way, toward the backward L, is right? Doesn't help. It's practically foolproof, and I still get it wrong. I'll hold up my hands like that sometimes (yes, in public), study 'em real good—brows furrowed, the tip of my tongue sticking out in concentration—and then turn the wrong direction. I don't know what's broken in my head, but it's seriously embarrassing.

Right after my wife and I first moved to California, I was driving back home from San Francisco for what should have been a leisurely one-hour jaunt. Sounds easy, right? Yeah, well this is me—Mr. Directionally Challenged—we're talking about. Three hours later, I had spent $35 on various tolls, bridges, and other forms of Californian Money Extraction Schemery™ only to find out what I should have known three hours earlier—I was lost.

I called my wife from a place I had never heard of. I looked for a sign, any sign, that would help me find some semblance of where I was. When I found one (reading "Milpitas"), I absolutely butchered the pronunciation as "Muh-lip-i-tiss" (?!?). Sarah began to laugh. Then she began to swear. And then finally she began to weep. Completely confused by the female emotional process (maybe we'll just save that for another book), I asked her what was wrong. Turns out this "Muh-lip-i-tiss" place is over an hour away from both where I live and San Francisco.

Four hours later—and $35 poorer—I finally made it home. My lovely bride, dehydrated from all the crying, welcomed me at the door. (Well, "welcomed" may be a little gracious.)

"Ya know that *Driving Miss Daisy* lady? Yeah, she knew what she was doing," I declared.

I Need Help!

It was because of directionally challenged incidents like this that I invited a special woman named Karen into my life. Over time,

Karen has become one of my best friends and trusted allies. She regularly joins me when I go out for dinner with my wife and children and has even tagged along with us on our vacations.

You'd think my wife would be jealous of the time Karen and I spend together, but Sarah is actually relieved whenever Karen accompanies me on a business trip. Sometimes she even insists I take Karen with me and reminds me when I forget. This is because Karen Jacobsen single-handedly helped me overcome the problem of always being lost . . . and also because Karen Jacobsen is definitely not trying to steal Sarah's husband. She's the voice of Garmin GPS devices, and right now—as you read this—she is giving directions to over 25 million people on this planet.

Karen (some refer to her as Australian Karen) was chosen by Garmin as their "spokesperson" based on her soothing accent and calming voice. I don't think I need to explain in great detail why Karen needs to have a soothing accent. Let's be honest: We've spent some of our worst, most pathetic moments in life engaged in one-way yelling contests with Karen. (No? Just me?) All it takes is a couple of directional miscommunications, and our conversation starts to look like the kind of civil dispute where cops should step in.

> KAREN: Turn right ahead.
> ME: There is no right, you robotic witch!
> KAREN: Turn left.
> ME: You lie! That takes me to a desert! Where are you taking me, you foul woman?!
> KAREN: You have reached your destination.
> ME: No, it didn't! You take me that route again and I'll take you to *your* final destination.

Or, what's even more common . . .

> KAREN: Turn left.
> ME: (Turns right.)
> KAREN: Recalculating . . .
> ME: ARRRGGHHHHHHHHH!

Usually I realize I'm overreacting and drawing alarmed looks from fellow travelers (*Why is that weird little man yelling at a plastic box suction-cupped to his windshield?*). Then I start to feel bad and try to smooth things over with Karen. You know, sing her a little Boyz II Men: "I'm sorry, baby. I didn't mean those horrible things I said to you. Please don't tell me to recalculate again. I just want to be on route with you. Ahhh, yeah." After all, I need this woman to stick around for the long haul.

So, how does GPS work? I have no idea, and honestly I don't care. Satellites, geolocators, beaming signals, triangulation, yadda yadda. All I know is it wields some kind of magic above my pay grade. And it is a crucial help in figuring out where in the world I am.

Not too long ago, I was joking with a group of friends about my "guidance issue" when one of my buddies asked me an interesting question: "How can you be so completely and eternally lost in the real world when it comes to physical directions, yet when it comes to your career, you know every single step you're about to take?"

And he's right. I admit that I am rarely, if ever, lost when talking about my job and my goals for the future. I somehow ended up with a strong internal guidance system when it came to making life decisions, but got disastrously shorted when it came to my geographic location.

His comment made me wonder if either of these skills were learnable. For example, was it possible to improve my awareness of my surroundings or strengthen my memory to become a better navigator of my physical world? (So far, not much luck there, I should warn you.) And, more importantly, how could someone acquire or nurture a sense of *inner* direction?

I had to believe there were principles and perspectives that, if applied, served as a type of GPS for your life that could provide orientation over the course of a person's career as well.

Can GPS Help Me Find My Dream Job?
I imagined, then, what a vocational GPS system would look like. I envisioned someone typing in his or her coordinates.

> *Starting Location: Taco Bell Employee*
> *Final Location: Self-Employed Graphic Designer*

Or maybe someone could even speak to this device just as an iPhone user talks to Siri. The thought of adding advice functions to the Siri app fascinated me momentarily, and my ADD took over.

> ME: Siri, where am I?
> SIRI: Here's your current location . . .

Up pops a page that pinpoints exactly where I am. I can even see an outline of my house and my favorite coffee shop down the street that I've bookmarked.

> ME: Siri, how do I get to Chicago?
> SIRI: Here are directions to Chicago.

Like magic, Siri shows me three possible routes to downtown Chicago from my front doorstep. This is the power of GPS! It's brilliant! Next step. Can Siri help me manage the bizarre path toward my dream job? Let's see how far the rabbit hole goes . . .

> ME: How do I find my dream job?
> SIRI: Sorry, I don't understand.
> ME: Siri, how do I become successful?

(By the way, this is an actual conversation.)

> SIRI: Hmm . . . Let me think. I don't know that. Would you
> like me to search the Web for it?
> ME: What am I good at?
> SIRI: No comment.
> ME: What do you think I should do for a profession?
> SIRI: I really couldn't say.
> ME: Should I open my own bakery?
> SIRI: I think you should sleep on it.
> ME: Should I become an accountant?
> SIRI: I found a number of accountants. Twenty-one of them
> are fairly close to you.
> ME: What will make me happy?
> SIRI: I don't know what you mean by, "What will make me
> happy?"

Obviously, this could go on for quite a while (and it did). But I think her last comment above is the truest answer she'd ever offer the user: "I don't know what you mean."

She's a digital phantom, a bunch of well-organized 1s and 0s.

Although she appears to have some reasoning functions, she is actually just spitting back preprogrammed responses defined by her makers in Cupertino, California. Siri doesn't actually know what will make you happy, and thus the more specific the user's questions get, the more her answers will fail to satisfy.

Daydreaming about technology aside, the real question, then, is how can a person—how can *you*—know where you are along the route to where you want to be? What choices and turns will lead to happiness?

I am learning a lot about this, but in order to explain some of the insights that have helped me make sense of my world, I have to take you back in time to a place from your childhood schooling that many of you dreaded and are scarred by: Algebra II.

I know it's painful, but it's worth it. First, think back with me. I'm guessing you dealt with this issue sometime during an Algebra II lesson, or while studying vectors in physics.

Oftentimes, the lesson began with a teacher instructing you to take out a piece of paper and draw a dot. Then he or she would ask the class, "Where is that dot?"

If you're anything like me, you were usually confused by this question. "Umm, it's on my paper?"

Then some others would try and guess, "On my desk?" "In this classroom?" "Is the dot in Flint, Michigan?" "The United States!" "Is the dot in the Western Hemisphere!?" "Earth!"

How do you go about explaining where something as small and abstract as a dot is?

The trick questionery and random guessing continued for what seemed like eternity while you prayed for a fire drill to interrupt the dot-locating madness you were sure you would never need in real life until, finally, the teacher caved and gave you the answer.

He or she had you draw a simple two-line graph with both an

x- (horizontal) and y- (vertical) axis. Then you were asked to draw points along the axis and to label them with numbers. The center of the graph was 0. And as you moved away from the graph the number changed. If you moved to points up or to the right of the center, the numbers increased by increments of one. If you went down or to the left (into negative space), they decreased by increments of one, represented by negative numbers.

Suddenly, with this little bit of information, you had some language and methodology for telling someone else where a dot was.

If the answer is (4, 7), you know that the point is 4 units to the right of 0 and 7 units up from 0. Or you could note (−1, −9) and know that now you are moving 1 unit left into "negative space" on the graph and down to −9. Kind of like that old board game Battleship. B7. D3.

This is the same sort of basic math that an actual GPS device uses to calculate your geographic location.

Of course, eventually, you learn there is one small add-on. When you have an x-axis and a y-axis, you are only operating in two-dimensional space. But all real objects, like your car or Disney World or Wrigley Field or your favorite Thai restaurant, exist in three-dimensional space. To address this, your math teacher would've probably added the z-axis, which indicated not the side-to-side or up-and-down locations, but "front-to-back" coordinates as well.

With the x-, y-, and z-axis points and a graph big enough that we can all refer to it; you can locate anything, anywhere in the world. In fact, I started thinking more and more about physical locations and realized that nearly every location is found in reference to not two, not four, but exactly three points.

Think about it. If you wanted to find your location anywhere on the planet, you would need longitude, latitude, and altitude.

If you were to go to a concert, you'd need to know section, row, and seat number.

To find a quote in a book, you'd need to know the title, page number, and line number.

Where do you live? That's measured by the city, street, and house number.

To find your seat on the plane? Gate, row, and seat number.

Now that you're registering this little factoid, you can probably think of other instances where you need three pieces of information to locate something precisely.

With all that in mind, I invite you to imagine something with me. What would happen if you only had two of those numbers? How frustrating would it be to find these locations?!

What if you had to flip through every page of a book because you didn't have the page number a quote was located on? Or search every home on the block because you didn't have the house number?

All these thoughts of algebra and calculating locations using three data points led me to two things: (1) an unusual feeling of pride and surprise that I'd remembered anything at all from my high school math classes; (2) the development of a useful tool for determining a person's "vocational location."

Finding Your Vocational Location

Let's clarify what I'm talking about when I say "vocational location." Vocational location is not the same thing as your dream job. It's not even the route you take to get there. Yes, it involves your dream job and is useful for planning your route, but, ultimately, GPS does one thing: It tells you where you are. This is where every journey must begin.

Before you jump, you must know where you are.

Introducing . . .

The Jump GPS

Similarly to the way coordinates on the x-, y-, and z-axis help us locate a dot, I believe there are three pieces of information that help us figure out where we are on the journey toward our dream job.

> *The X factor is your* present.
> *The Y factor is your* past.
> *The Z factor is your* future.

My theory suggests that if you are having trouble figuring out your vocational location, it's because you are having trouble with one or more of the above axis points. Until you can map out the details of all three of those points, you will continue to be lost. It's the same as driving around with a GPS that isn't plugged in.

If you really want to make forward progress on the seven steps toward your dream job, you must—and I can't stress this enough—you must know your current location.

The Y Factor: Your Past (Experience)

I love that the "Y factor" sounds like the "why factor," since this axis is all about figuring out why you are the way you are.

This is the opportunity for you to look back at everything that you've experienced and ask yourself that question: "Why?" "Why did this happen to me?" "Why did I choose that?" "Why have I never tried this?" "Why was I forgotten?" "Why was I loved so much?" "Why did I not make the team?" "Why did I end up being great at the French horn?" "Why was I verbally abused as a child?" "Why did I grow up with such a competitive spirit?" Don't just catalog what's happened—question it. Try to understand it.

Remember, the point of asking why is to figure out how you ended up where you are today and where you'd like to end up.

When some people talk about your "past" what they really mean is your baggage. That's an important part of the Y factor, but it's not the whole thing.

Think of the Y factor as what has happened in your life up until now. This includes everything from when and where and to whom you were born, where you went to school, what you did in school, and every job you've ever had. Your Y factor is your CV in the original Latin sense—your "course of life." It's where you've been and what you've learned, what you've done and what's been done to you.

When you think about your past, remember that your entire life so far—as it happened and as you remember it—is all in the past. Technically, the sentence you just read is in the past.

Okay, so thinking like that can get overwhelming pretty quickly. But you'll never figure out your vocational location if you don't examine your past.

It may seem strange to start in the past. After all, you picked up this book to think about moving toward your future. But as much as people sometimes fear the movie-esque therapy couch and the flashbacks to miserable childhood moments, your past is absolutely key in preparing to jump and is probably inextricably tied to your dream job.

Specifically, you'll want to look at two things: (1) how you've suffered and what you've learned from it; (2) what you've enjoyed more than anything else. Let me tell you how that worked for me.

When I was a teenager and I first started seriously thinking about what I wanted to do with my life, my dreams—and my determination to reach them—were deeply affected by what I'd been through up until that point. I'd spent a huge part of my life in failure, frustration, depression, and rebellion. But I was (successfully, with a lot of help and patience) working to overcome all that. I knew from past experience that people thought I was funny. I knew I enjoyed speaking to large groups of people, and I knew people generally enjoyed it when I did. Looking at where I'd been and what I'd learned about myself and about life, I realized what I wanted to do: I wanted to use public speaking as a platform for helping kids like me.

In that moment, it all came together and I suddenly felt as though I had a special calling and a unique role to play.

Yes, some of my past is hard to look back on. And it does me no good to dwell on the bad emotions that swirl around it. But I owe a lot to my past. My past taught me what I was good at and what I had to offer the world. It's given me an incredibly powerful story to share, a way to connect with and relate to others who have suffered or are suffering, and proof to show them that change is possible, that there is hope.

Lean in because this is super-important. Without these low points, my message would not and could not reach the audience I serve. If I erased my past it would change the whole story. Literally, the *only* reason I can do what I do today is *because* of my past. My past didn't merely influence the kind of dreams I had for my life; in very real ways, my past made those dreams possible.

Your story—your Y factor—won't look anything like mine. You've been shaped by different experiences, suffered through and overcome different problems, and found enjoyment in vastly different activities. But, regardless of what specific events have shaped your life, it's important to ask how they have—or how they can—drive you toward something great.

The Z Factor: Your Future (Goals)

The Z factor represents your future. In the same way that all the other letters in the alphabet lead up to Z, everything in your past and the choices in your present lead up to your future.

Think of the Z factor as where you hope to go from here. This axis is all about your goals, dreams, ambitions, hopes, and sense of calling. Z is the target. Z is where you're pouring your heart, your drive, and your passion. Z is what you're aiming for when you jump.

We'll talk more about the Z factor in Part Two.

The X Factor: Your Present (Reality)

Between what's happened up until now and where you hope to go from here is a single moment in time, a moment that holds the potential to change everything. It's called the present. This is your X factor.

Or, in the words of every motivational speaker ever . . .

Now is the first moment of the rest of your life.

I know, I know . . . it's a cheesy saying, but there's a reason why almost every coach or teacher or inspiring leader has a message that captures this concept. It's entirely true.

The x-axis is where you live and breathe and make decisions, like whether or not to jump. X marks the spot—this moment in time. Today is where the magic happens.

NOW could be the moment where, if you want to be a writer, you finally sit your butt down in the chair and start writing. If you're an athlete, NOW is the time to go practice. If you're an actor, NOW is the time to prepare for that audition you've been dreading. If you want a job, NOW is the time to get on Craigslist or get online to follow up about that informational interview.

NOW might be the moment where you end a negative relationship. Or maybe it's your chance to go and ask for forgiveness from a friend. It might be the time to quit your job and make the jump. It might be the time to enroll in a new class to take you one tiny baby step closer to your ideal future. It might be the time to take up a new hobby or to start losing that weight you promised to lose this year.

You have to figure out how to break down the future you imagine into measurable and manageable goals you can act on right away. We'll take a further look at this in step five, but I cannot stress how powerful—and critical—the X factor is in this formula.

What you do in the present will make or break the whole equation.

Calculating . . .

You can always calculate your personal vocational GPS by triangulating these three points: your past, future, and present.

The equation looks something like this: Based on [these things] in the past (Y factor), I'm choosing to do [this] in the present (X factor) in order to accomplish [this] in the future (Z factor).

$$Y + X = Z$$

When you wake up and realize one day that you're offtrack, power up your GPS and figure out what went wrong. Maybe you had a new insight about your past or a new defining experience. Maybe your goals for the future have changed. Or maybe you've simply been making choices in the present that have led you the wrong way.

Knowing exactly where you've been, where you're going, and where you are in between helps you maintain vocational

direction at a time when people tend to feel lost, scared, and unprepared.

Congratulations, wayfarer. You now know the secret equation
to finding yourself.

Well, partially, anyway . . .

Finding Yourself (Part Two)

At some point in your life, you are going to have to confront yourself. You might as well do it now.

—ALEXANDRA ROBBINS

There's a second part to finding yourself beyond knowing your vocational location, and, really, it's even more basic. Not only is it critical to know *where* you are before you jump, you must also know *who* you are.

The question at hand is one of identity, and it's a question I come back to over and over and over again, because, over and over and over again, I see people gloss over it and wind up in a world of hurt and confusion.

Why is this issue so important? Because your identity lies at the core of who you believe you are and what you think you're capable of. It's the truth (or lie) that generates (or undermines) your self-confidence, and it's inextricably linked to your dream.

It goes like this:

Who You Are → What You Want → How to Get It

Or, to play it in reverse, we can't get you through the seven steps if you don't know what you want, and you're never going to know what you want if you don't know who you are.

You cannot know what you want until you have a solid sense of who you are. Don't believe me?

Imagine for a second that your dream job is a gift you'd like to give to yourself. Ever try buying a gift for someone you don't really know? It's a total shot in the dark, and usually ends with a gift card to iTunes or something kind of generic that "everybody" likes. The gift doesn't really have any special meaning or value to the person.

If you want to give a specific, personally tailored gift to someone—something that's particularly thoughtful and meaningful that they're absolutely sure to love and appreciate—you really have to know the person first. (Sorry, "personalizing" that e-card with their name doesn't count.)

Same deal with your dream job. You'll never know if it's a good fit for you if you don't really know your personal tastes. The last thing you want to do is to go through all the trouble and hard work of making the jump only to land in some generic "dream job" with your name slapped on it. Enjoy your monogrammed sweatshirt.

Skip this task at your own peril. Even if you work through all the seven steps, I promise you, you'll wind up right back where you started—disappointed, confused, and ready for a change—if you never take the time now to deal with the issue of identity. Except next time through you'll be older. Bummer.

At some point in your life you're going to have to face yourself. You've got to get behind all the protective layers—material goods, advanced degrees, expectations, pressures, and postures you've internalized—and confront your naked identity.

The people who don't do this or put it off will never successfully make the jump to where they want to be, because they don't even know what that is or where it can be found. They'll just hop around or settle into unhappiness until a midlife crisis overwhelms them and opens up the whole issue again.

As millennials, you and I may be part of the first generation that's expected to end up worse off than our parents financially, but we're probably also the first generation with the time and tools to address the issues of identity head-on in early adulthood instead of decades down the road, after we're deeply invested in a life we never wanted. This means we've got a much better shot at living out our dreams and finding satisfaction in our work than previous generations. I call that a win. Given a choice between riches or happiness, the smart person picks happiness every time.

Identity Affects Everything

Who you are—or, more specifically, who you think you are— affects everything else in your life. Most of you will have guessed by now, since I've dropped hints here and there, that I had a pretty rough childhood and early adulthood. What you may not know is that, like many other kids, I allowed my past—my Y factor—to completely define me. Abandonment taught me I wasn't wanted. Abuse taught me I wasn't valuable. Neglect taught me I wasn't important. Bullying taught me I deserved it. And I believed it all. I allowed those experiences to define who I was, and that completely dictated who I thought I could be in the future.

Once, I distinctly remember a guy telling me—yelling at me—that I was just a punk, orphan, foster kid, and that was all I'd ever be. Nothing more. Nothing less. I can still see the look on his face. Looking back, it felt a lot like the scene from *Aladdin* where Prince Achmed snarls at Aladdin, "You are a worthless street rat. You were born a street rat. You'll die a street rat. And only your fleas will mourn you." Who says that kind of thing to a kid?

Words like that deeply affected me. I believed him. I believed that's who I was—a punk, orphan, foster kid—and that's all I'd ever be.

An identity like that can put a damper on your outlook—on your Z factor—if you know what I mean. Guess what I hoped for in my future? Nothing. In my most honest moments, I wanted to die.

Guess how that affected my here and now, my X factor?

You got it. I acted out. I made decisions consistent with who I thought I was and where I thought I was going: Every day, I chose to be a punk, orphan, foster kid. I goofed off in class, picked fights, ran my mouth, disobeyed my foster parents, and flaunted the law. I nearly destroyed myself.

But hear me now, because this is important: THAT'S WHAT I WANTED. When you hear me tell this story, don't think that the trouble was that I wasn't living my dream. That *was* my dream—my Z factor. I wanted to kill myself. And each and every action I took was taking me closer and closer to my goal.

Thankfully, I never got there.

Care to take a guess about what turned me around?

If you guessed a shift in "identity," you get a gold star.

For me, it took the loving patience of my foster parents and a handful of caring teachers to finally help me see that all those lessons I'd learned from horrible experiences in my past were lies and that they didn't have to define me. What my Prince Achmed yelled at me wasn't entirely true. Sure, I spent a lot of time acting like a punk, orphan, foster kid . . . but I didn't have to. That wasn't my fate. I could be a diamond in the rough.

I began to accept my past and started pulling good cues from my Y factor—observations about what I was good at, what made me unique, what I loved, and what I believed. This completely changed the way I thought about the future, which completely changed what I wanted to do with my life (a concept that had never really occurred to me before), which completely changed the choices I made every day.

I didn't know it at the time, but I was making the jump.

A few short years after getting a grip on my identity, I was getting paid to speak to classrooms full of hundreds—and then thousands—of kids about how to overcome adversity. I was doing what I was made to do, instead of throwing my life away.

Statistically, I should've ended up homeless or dead or in prison; instead, I help change the world.

I'm living proof that changing your identity—changing your perception of yourself--changes *everything*.

So let's get down to brass tacks.

Who Are You?

It's a simple question, weighing in at just three words. It's probably one of the most basic questions in the entire world. But it's also a question that is a lot harder to answer than it seems. And only you can answer it. You can't outsource this identity thing.

Well, you can, but then you're just letting some ill-willed mercenary pirate character captain your ship while you take a nap belowdecks.

If you don't figure out who you are, someone else will try to tell you. And my fear is that if you listen to them for long enough, like I did, you'll start to believe them.

Don't let that happen. Your identity is for *you* to decide and discover. It is something you have to own for yourself.

By the way, it's okay if you don't figure everything out right away. Discovering who you are is a lifelong process and certain things are going to change or become more or less important over time. I'm not who I was when I was seventeen. I won't be exactly the same when I'm seventy. That's good.

The important thing is to find what's true about you—something you can hang your hat on and test your dreams against. Here are some basic questions to get you started on your journey of self-enlightenment.

First, What Makes You Unique?

This is an easy place to start since it can be a little more concrete. Think about your experiences, your quirks, your unconscious habits, or even physical traits.

But don't get too hung up on enumerating your differences. You're not unique like a snowflake; you're unique like a person. You'll have a lot of things in common with a lot of people. Believe it or not, these specific commonalities—experiences or characteristics or propensities that you share with certain groups and not others—make you unique, too. Maybe you're introverted or extroverted. Maybe you like the details, or maybe you like the big picture. Perhaps you had a great home growing up, or maybe, like me, not so much. Maybe you can see connections that other people can't; maybe you're creative or artistic. Maybe you're good with numbers. No matter what makes you unique, there are characteristics that do.

Second, What Do You Love?

What makes you happy or gets you excited? What can't you stop talking about? What thoughts do you keep coming back to? What warms you up inside?

Pay attention to those things, activities, and situations, because they are what you love. Some of that may change over time, but a lot of it won't, so take notes. Same thing goes for the stuff you don't like—the stuff that annoys you and bums you out and makes you want to wear sackcloth and ashes. Some people don't like the business side of things. Some don't like day-to-day mundaneness. Some people hate being trapped inside an office. Others don't like the instability that often comes with trying something new. Whatever it might be for you, listen to it. Listen to what gets you excited; but also listen to the things that suck the life out of you.

Third, What Are You Good At?

It's important to recognize when you feel strong and when you don't. Whether you want to believe it, you have certain skills, talents, and gifts that set you apart. You are good at something. You may not be the absolute BEST in the world at this thing, but you're miles ahead of most people. You probably don't even realize you're good at it because it comes so easily that you don't even notice.

Figure out what makes you feel strong, capable, and fulfilled. Write them down and pursue those things.

Fourth, What Do You Believe?

I'm not going to get into this too deeply, but I am going to encourage you to. Faith and spirituality—whether you're an unequivocal atheist, a devout Roman Catholic, or a searching mystic—plays a huge role in shaping your identity. Beliefs tend to be very deep-seated and exert a lot of influence over your dreams and how you go about pursuing them.

If you've never sat down to think about it, take a few days (or years) to really think through some of Life's Ultimate Questions—the kinds of questions that keep philosophers up at night. Where did we come from? What is the meaning of life? What happens after death? You know, little brainteasers like that.

This Is Just the Beginning

I hope that didn't wear you out too much, because I have news: When it comes to facing your identity, these four basic questions barely scratch the surface.

If you want to see how far down the rabbit hole goes, I'd recommend picking up a copy of Don Richard Riso and Russ Hudson's *The Wisdom of the Enneagram*. Don't judge the book by its cover; it's an ugly old thing, but it's chock-full of knowledge. Again, this book isn't the final word on your identity—no book ever can be, really—but it ought to jumpstart a lot of healthy introspection that could take you a few steps closer to finding yourself.

Once you have your identity as a foundation, it's time to begin our journey.

Life Lesson Number One: "Shake Well. Settling Is Natural"

Many a false step is made standing still.

—A JONES SODA BOTTLE CAP

So, here you are. You've done some hard thinking about who you are and who you aspire to be and have found your location—that pulsing blue dot somewhere between your past and the future you want.

Now that you know where you stand, we're ready to dig a little deeper. Knowing your location is critical—you have to start there. But finding your starting location is just the first (and usually easiest) part of a journey.

Let's try a quick exercise. Go sit in your car and turn on your GPS, or stand still and pull out your smartphone and fire up the Google Maps app and find your current location. See that little car icon or that little dot? That's you. That's where you are.

Notice anything?

It doesn't move. On its own, a GPS pinpoints your location and tells you where you are. It doesn't move you from point A to point B. *It reacts to your movement.* It can lay out a path for you, but it doesn't force you to follow it. You're still free to turn right when it says left is the way you want to go. Even more significantly, you're free to sit there.

Which is probably why you're still at your current location and not living the life and working the job you wish you were. You haven't moved.

Which brings us to an important truth.

We All Struggle with Forward Motion

When I speak, part of my core message is refusing to settle for the ordinary. That was the essence of my earlier book, *The Teen's Guide to World Domination,* where I wrote about what it takes to be a "hero" and explained how to identify and fight off everyday "villains"—ghosts, ninjas, pirates, robots, vampires, zombies, and puppies (long story)—that contend for control of a teen's world. I wanted to tell young people stories that would offer hope as they attempt to overcome the struggles of being a teen. But, most importantly, I wanted to show them that living an above average life is possible.

In fact, that same idea is one of the driving forces behind this book as well. Refusing to settle is one of those stories within me that kicks and screams and demands to be told. I believe that sharing this message is part of my calling, and getting paid for it is part of my dream job.

The tricky part is that I've shared this idea—that you don't have to settle for ordinary—hundreds, maybe *thousands* of times. But I still find myself forgetting to apply this lesson in my own life, even as I'm saying it in front of a roomful of people.

What's my deal?!

Hear me here: This is something I still struggle with. I've been working my dream job since high school, and I've written books and hosted my own TV shows. Yet I still struggle with forward motion. I'm still in danger of settling for the ordinary.

I've seen enough failures, even in the lives of successful people, to know that all of us have to maintain our awareness and commitment to choosing the best life, no matter how accomplished we become.

This has been a problem for me ever since I started developing a career as a speaker, writer, and TV host. I want to continue to pursue a remarkable life, but it is way easier to stop pushing toward the best and become lazy in a comfort zone with the things I'm doing now.

A few years back, though, I learned something that helped me maintain the mind-set I needed. We'll call this life lesson number one.

Life Lesson Number One: "Shake Well. Settling Is Natural"

This is something I didn't really put words to or fully realize until several years ago, and it's number one not because I learned it first but because it's a lesson that's particularly relevant to people's wrestling with the nagging desire to jump.

Typically for me, life lessons show up after spending the night in jail or sobbing, with streams of spit and snot hitting nearby loved ones in the face. But, on occasion, life is generous and tosses me a slow-softball pitch and begs me, pleads with me, to hit it out of the park.

Here's how it happened for me. I have a routine. Each morning I wake up extremely early and throw on my running clothes. I drive to meet up with my friends, the marathon crew—or as my friends call them, the Marathon Death Squad—and we run anywhere between five and twenty miles, depending on our schedule. Years ago, in an effort to get my life in better shape, I decided I wanted to run a marathon, so I started running with this same group of people, who have become my dear friends, mentors in different areas of life, and accountability partners.

When I started, I knew little of what I was getting myself into, especially considering running is essentially a cult practice to those who have caught the bug. But, all in all, runners are some of the best people to hang around with because, by nature, they are very disciplined. For that reason, I never could have become a runner on my own. It's far too easy to sleep through an alarm when you are the only person accountable to your training schedule. When you know there is going to be a group of people waiting for you every morning, giving you a hard time if you wuss out, then the motivation gets a little stronger.

Especially when some of the people waiting for you and your wussy running shoes to show up are tiny women old enough to be your mother.

One early morning, keeping pace with my daily routine, I made my way into the kitchen to stuff a few calories into my body before the day's long jog. Bleary-eyed and gnawing on a banana, I fumbled around in the fridge for my Green Goodness juice and went to pour myself a glass. As I held the bottle, I happened to notice, as if for the first time, some text written just below the cap. It read:

Shake Well. Settling Is Natural.

Now, I've probably read that text and obeyed its instructions by shaking the juice bottle a thousand times. Shaking juice bottles is a habit most of us picked up before we were tall enough to see over the kitchen counter. This habit is so deeply and subconsciously ingrained in some of us that I know people who shake their milk.

We usually shake our juice (or salad dressing, or whatever) without thinking about why. I guess I was kind of vaguely aware that the juice has all sorts of good ingredients in there that tend to separate when the bottle sits still in the fridge for a few hours; we've all seen how the heavier stuff in a bottle, like pulp, sinks to the bottom while some lighter elements rise to the top. I knew full well that to get the best possible glass of juice, I should shake it all up, mixing up all the tiny healthy particles before pouring it into my glass. But for some reason, after years of performing this routine, it didn't hit me until *this* morning how incredibly profound that simple phrase is.

My perspective on life had just been transformed by a bottle of juice.

"Settling Is Natural . . ."

Why did that simple statement nearly knock me over at 5:00 on a random Tuesday morning? Because in one sentence, it not only defined what I had to do if I intended to pursue my best self but also explained the reason why we often fail when trying to reach higher, perform better, or be above average.

I'd always spent a big chunk of my time reflecting on and talking about pursuing my best life, but there were still times I wondered why I didn't see more exciting and new things happening in my life. Suddenly, the juice label had spelled it out: Even good things, when left unattended for too long, tend to settle.

I recently read a book called *Iconoclast,* by Gregory Berns. It's a great book that talks about how "iconoclasts"—people like Richard Branson, Walt Disney, Steve Jobs, and Henry Ford—manage to think differently because they actually see the world differently. In the beginning of the book, Berns explains how our brains are biologically hardwired to fixate on efficiency. Why? He says that when we move outside our comfort zone, our brains have to start working much harder, which requires our bodies to expend more energy and increases our metabolic responses. Our brains and our bodies prefer to be at rest—to expend as little effort as possible to survive.

The primal caveman-type instincts in us hate the concept of "thinking harder" or "thinking differently" because all we want to do is survive, which means not expending too much energy, which requires finding more food. All we want to do is protect ourselves from being gored by a woolly mammoth or knocked out by Barney Rubble (our barbarian neighbor) with a club. While our modern-day situation bears little resemblance to the lives of our cave-dwelling hunter-gatherer ancestors, this desire for efficiency still exists in each of us.

In biology, this idea is expressed by the principle of homeostasis, which comes from a Greek word meaning "to remain stable." It's the tendency toward a relatively stable equilibrium. Our bodies are designed to self-regulate, with a whole slew of interdependent physiological systems and processes working all the time to keep everything stable—from body temperature to blood sugar levels. In fact, biologically, your body hates instability so much that even relatively small deviations from its preferred state will actually kill you. If your core body temperature, normally somewhere around 98.6 degrees Fahrenheit, falls 12 degrees or rises even half of that, your body starts to shut down fast.

Now, homeostasis is a good thing; you'd be dead without those physiological regulatory processes. I don't mean to suggest that all forms of stability and equilibrium are bad. I just think it's interesting that virtually everything inside of you *naturally resists change.*

Unless I intentionally pick up my life and give it a good shake, it starts to settle. Everything starts to separate and taste watery. And that's natural. Settled is our default state of being. Settled is ordinary. Left to our own devices, settling is inevitable.

"Shake Well"

Moving toward your best self requires some shaking up, some unsettling, or—practically speaking—some conscious decisions to change the way you're investing your attention. But your brain is naturally yelling out, "No! Let me be lazy and efficient!" in the same way your body might resist you as you head to workout at the gym.

If you pause to identify the times you feel most creative— when your brain is most alive—it's probably when you are taking in new information. I know I get my best ideas when I'm traveling in a new country or even lying on a beach. I can also be inspired by going to a museum or watching a new movie, hiking through the woods or jogging through a new neighborhood. New sights, sounds, languages, architecture—almost anything new—can shake up your brain enough to unsettle it and make it work harder. And when your brain works harder, it grows in its capacity to start seeing the world around you in different ways.

I bet you can go back in time and see the difference between moments when you shook it up versus the moments you decided to settle.

One of the first times I remember shaking up my life was when I decided to run for senior class president.

Now, if you read my first book or have heard me speak, you know I wasn't the best student in school. I wasn't that guy who wins all the awards, has a 4.0 GPA, and quarterbacks the football team. In fact, I was the complete opposite of that guy. Still, I'd managed to carve out a comfortable little niche for myself over time. By senior year, I was pretty comfortable. I felt settled.

When I chose to take a risk and run for senior class president, I chose to put my head on the chopping block of disappointment and criticism. Typically, when I look back and talk about this experience, I say the whole thing was just done as a joke, but I'd be lying if I said I didn't want to win. I'd spent enough of my life as a loser by that point that the prospect of a humiliating defeat made my gut churn. Saying it was a joke was just my way of protecting myself against disappointment. I cared. I wanted it badly enough to try. But I wasn't about to take it so seriously and so personally that losing would undo me.

I was a class clown, so, naturally, my campaign slogan was, "Shipp Happens." When the votes were tallied, I was relieved that the Shipp definitely had happened. I won.

I'd shaken things up. It was a serious risk for me socially, but by reaching out and trying something new, I was able to reposition myself within my high school. Of course, it also looked great on my college applications and helped me get into the University of Central Oklahoma, which is where I ended up meeting my wife, who is now the mother of my children. You never know where a simple shake might take you.

I was discussing this whole idea of shaking life up with a buddy of mine when he told me about one epic shake-up earlier in his life. Looking back, he still laughs as he remembers how he pulled this off. He was an aspiring filmmaker, was just barely out of college, and was looking for work.

My friend had heard that a nonprofit organization in North Carolina was looking for some fund-raising films to be made overseas. It sounded like an awesome opportunity, so he gave his life a little shake and made an inquiry. The organization requested a proposal from him, same as they did with all companies vying to be hired. He didn't have much (read: any) experience writing successful proposals at this point, so this was probably a little intimidating. Here was this unestablished college grad trying to pitch himself against veteran companies.

Even though he was still considered an amateur in the field, my buddy decided to shake again and go all in. He put together a really strong proposal and even got on the phone with one of the leaders of the organization.

She was very nice but was up front: "Hiring is a decision that can only be made by the executive staff, and, unfortunately, they don't all get together very often."

When my friend asked when the executive staff would be together next, she admitted that there was a fund-raising banquet the next week, "but there will be so much going on, I can't even guarantee they'll get time to meet."

To her credit, the lady was honest at a level that would've probably encouraged most people to call off the hunt, settle down, and wait for the elusive "next time." But my buddy resisted the impulse to settle.

"I'll be there," he told her.

The woman didn't even know how to respond. She quickly reiterated that there was little to no chance of their agreeing to a meeting on such short notice and that this trip could very well be a complete waste of his time. Presented with an opportunity (and sound reasons) to settle, my friend insisted on shaking harder: "That's fine. Just let them know I'll be there with my proposal. If there's anything you can do to help me gather them into the same room, I'd really appreciate it."

Since he was fresh out of school, my friend had very little money, but he worked out a plan to drive twelve hours to North Carolina and stay with a college friend. He put on his only suit jacket and attended the banquet for the nonprofit with no guarantee of a meeting. Finally, the woman (who, let's face it, probably felt bad he'd driven so far) managed to convince the executives to gather in a conference room the next day to hear his proposal. He presented and, by some miracle, won them over.

Five months later, he was on a whirlwind five-week tour

traveling to ten countries from Morocco to Jordan capturing stories for the organization. Not bad for an early job as an aspiring
filmmaker! My friend took the chance to risk his time and
money to drive twelve hours for a meeting that wasn't even on
the books. But it worked. This shake-up not only provided an
amazing life opportunity but also served as an incredible inter-
national addition to my friend's film reel and led to work on future projects. By shaking instead of settling, he moved forward
toward his dream job.

I think most of us, including myself, want to be that kind of
person—the kind of person who dares to shake things up.

You will always feel the desire to settle in your personal life,
relationships, career, and all aspects of life, because it's natural.
But that tendency to settle is nothing that a brisk shake can't
fix.

If you're anything like me, you might start to feel like a failure
in the moments you're tempted to give into laziness. It's really
important to know that everyone, including me, fights that battle
every single day. It doesn't matter what you're *tempted* to do;
what matters is whether or not you give into the temptation.

This is the struggle you have ahead of you. It is up to you and
you alone. Settle or shake. When we choose to shake it up, we
are inviting new, unknown, and (most likely) fear-inducing experiences into our lives. But these are also the moments when we
decide to take on risk, to steer into the waves, to choose the road
less traveled—to live! The people we admire or are encouraged
by on a daily basis haven't "settled" into success. They got there—
and stay there—because they shake it up.

If you are afraid to make any big moves to shake up your life,
you may need to incorporate this principle into your life in smaller
ways before you invite it into your career path. The plan to Jump
Ship is a serious decision with massive effects on your life. I

guarantee it will require you to shake it up again and again. Start practicing now.

One of the simplest things you can do to start this process is to create a small note reminding you to "shake well," because "settling is natural" or to "shake or settle." Put it where you'll see it often, maybe on a bathroom mirror, your dashboard, your fridge, your desk at work, or your laptop or phone wallpaper.

This simple phrase invites a decision. It reminds you of your options in the everyday moments that make up your life. Break your routines or start a new routine. Do the hard thing. Make the extra effort. You may begin to shake it up by making a conscious decision to show kindness instead of road rage. You may go out of your way to serve another person instead of looking to be served. You may choose to give away your lunch to someone who needs it more than you. Your "shaking up" may begin with something as basic as caring enough to return your cart to the cart stall at the grocery store.

These practical exercises in shaking it up, as simple as they may seem, are important. One sentence on a bottle of juice has the potential to change your entire life and give you the courage to Jump Ship.

Now go and shake it like a Polaroid picture.

> **Reflection—Sue Fletcher** *Sue Fletcher loves to bake cupcakes. Her friends love her cupcakes. Everyone who's had Sue's cupcakes loves them. She thinks she has a gift for baking, and she imagines opening a bakery not just centered on flour and sugar and egg but on community. She's not quite ready to make the jump, though.*

It's 10:38 p.m. on a Sunday night and I've just finished watching a YouTube video on how to make a perfect toasted marshmallow frosting. I had to watch the video because I made some s'mores cupcakes and the recipe called for marshmallow frosting. I even went to Bed, Bath, and Beyond today to buy the kitchen torch that I needed to toast the frosting! I followed the recipe, to a T, but my marshmallow frosting came out soupy. After a bit of research on Google, I found a video detailing the steps for a perfect version. Thanks to YouTube, I now know what I did wrong. So, the cupcakes will wait in a container and I'll give it another go tomorrow.

This is what I do.

On the weekends, when most people are spending time with friends, watching movies, hanging by the pool, I am in my kitchen trying out the latest recipe that piques my interest. I spend countless hours in the kitchen whipping up wonderful concoctions, and then parade them into the office on Monday to wait for the momentary high that I get when someone describes how it tastes. I live for that moment.

Why?

Well, there's just something about baking for me. It's not about eating what I bake—although I enjoy that, too. For me, it's really about seeing a smile stretch across someone's face when they taste something that I've made. I've taken some ingredients and combined them in a particular order (which appeals to my mathematical mind), and the combination results in a moment when someone experiences joy. That, for me, is pure bliss.

I haven't been baking all my life, nor did I always love it. I remember finishing family meals with "something sweet" as my grandmother would always say, but I don't really recall having a penchant for the kitchen when I was young. Both of my grandmothers were fabulous bakers and my mom wasn't too shabby herself, but my real love for baking came when I first started dating my boyfriend, Bo.

Bo is from the South, where baking is part of a woman's DNA. He talked very fondly about the strawberry cake that one of his friend's moms used to make, and for some reason I wanted desperately to re-create that cake so that he could experience that same joy. Unfortunately, we lived in Colorado, where baking can be a bit of a challenge because of the altitude, but I tried and tried again, until one day he bit into a strawberry cupcake that I had baked, and there it was—the smile that assured me he had been transported back to enjoying the cupcake of his childhood.

I was hooked.

I went on to try recipe after recipe and figured out somewhere along the way that I was actually pretty good at this baking thing.

And thus the dream was born.

"You should open a bakery."

If I could count the times I've heard that.

And, the truth is, I would *love* to own a bakery.

When I was in college, I owned and operated a small coffee shop called the Java Well. It was run by volunteers from a campus group won over by the vision my friend and I dreamed up: to create a space for students to enjoy a cup of decent coffee, a baked good, some great art, live music, and conversation. We wanted a space where community could be built—a foundation for friendships and conversations that would, hopefully, create lifelong memories.

The experience of owning that coffee shop was one of the most important I've ever had. Sure, I learned a lot in my course work, but I learned more in the hours spent in the kitchen of that shop than I did in any classroom.

After graduating college, I went straight into the workforce, as was expected. I was a branch manager of a bank, a marketing manager for a large manufacturing company, an instructional designer for a sales training team. Then I took a drastic shift and worked in the nonprofit sector for a while in Colorado. There I met Bo, and my baking obsession began.

Bo and I have spent hours upon hours talking about the concept of a "third place." Here's how Stephen Hunter describes it:

> I'm not talking about winning and losing here, or races or sports or politics, but something far more important: the simple art of living your life in the real world. In that world, as someone has pointed out, all communities—and therefore all members of communities— need a "third place." It's not your home. It's not where you work. Those are the first two places.
>
> No, it's the place where you go to, um, be. ("Shear Gladness," The Washington Post, *September 13, 2002)*

It would seem that in order to build community, you need people, and in order to have people, you need a place. So why not make that place a bakery?

Good question. It's one that keeps me up at night.

So why don't I just go for it?

Well, right now I am working as the customer service and sales support director for a company called Sun Bum. I got this job through a connection from a previous job, and I really do like it. Honestly, I do. I work with a great group of people, and I'm really good at my job. The sales reps depend on me; my boss tells people that I run the place. I took a huge pay cut to start out there, but it is a company I believe will be huge in a few years. I'm happy to be a part of the team that will take it there.

My genuine hope is that I stay at Sun Bum long enough to make the six-figure salary I've always felt I deserve (don't we all think we deserve that?), pay off all my debt, and get myself in the financial position to be able to give this bakery idea a try.

That's all well and good, but why not just screw all that and do it now, you ask?

I think the plainest, most honest answer is fear and the unknown. What if I'm not good enough? What if no one wants to buy what I bake? What if it's a disaster? Where do I even begin, and how much money does it cost to actually open a bakery? What if I go into huge debt and can't make enough to pay the rent? If it doesn't work, then what do I dream about?

Somehow it's comforting to have your dream out there because then the only reason it hasn't come true is you haven't tried yet.

Ugh. That kinda sucks.

But it's true.

Life Lesson Number Two: The Enemy Within

I see a counselor.

In fact, I've seen counselors just about my entire life. When I was a kid it was sort of a mandatory part of being an at-risk teen in the foster care system. Plus, I was a steaming-hot mess. Concerned adults were always shaking their heads and saying I needed to see a counselor. Shouting back, "I already *do* see a counselor!" made me feel real good about myself, I'll tell you. Today, I see a counselor because I want to. I just know myself well enough to know that I need that unbiased insight and accountability in my life to help me stay grounded or process through things or tell me when I'm being an idiot.

I honestly think everybody should see a counselor once in a while. I learned early on that counselors are pretty clever.

Let me share a specific example:

> COUNSELOR: So, tell me, Josh, what would you like to see different as a result of meeting today?
> ME: Uh . . .

Usually, I'm not even thinking about what I want in a positive sense, so the question takes me off guard for a second. Well, I *don't* want to be unhappy, so I guess what I want to see differently is for . . . that . . . to . . . stop?

There was a period early on in our marriage when Sarah and I were getting into these stupid, petty fights. They were so miniscule that I honestly can't even remember what they were about, or even why they were such a big deal at the time. Seriously, no idea.

I remember talking to my therapist about this one day. "I think I need to be more kind." "She just needs to chill out." "I need to watch my words." "You know what I think? I think she needs to back off and stop nagging me."

Blah . . . blah . . . blah.

Then my counselor drops these questions: "Do these fights have a time-period pattern? Like before dinner? Or before you are going out of town?"

My heart sank: 99.9343234 percent of them happened the night before I was going out of town. Turns out that because I was abandoned as a kid, I had some—uh, ya know—abandonment issues. Shocking. The problem—the *real* problem—was that this fear of abandonment was creeping in and causing me to pick fights.

After all, it's easier to leave when the person you're leaving has annoyed you.

In the end, the root issue wasn't my tone; the root issue was how I perceive departures deep down inside of me. As I thought about it, I realized there was a pattern. I'm just not good at good-byes in general. I'd rather sneak out the back door at a party than go and give the official good-bye. And my wife is Italian, so she overcompensates and does a sixty-five-minute good-bye.

I needed to learn that just because I was leaving someone did *not* mean they were leaving me.

So how do I get rid of this problem?

"Truth is, Josh, you can't. These are the kinds of problems you can only manage. They never fully vanish. You have to learn to anticipate these kinds of situations, not let your emotions lie to you. Remind yourself what is really going on, and have a *preplanned,* different response."

Believe it or not, counseling situations like this happen all the time. In psychotherapy, conventional wisdom teaches that the "presenting problem"—what I walked into the session complaining about—is seldom the real problem. This is true for a number of reasons, but two reasons are especially common: people misidentify the real problem, or people conceal the real problem.

I've been guilty of doing both. I'm guessing you have, too. Therapists see this all the time—clients actively trying to solve the wrong problem, or throwing up smoke screens to distract from a problem they don't want to deal with. For example, a guy could "present" believing that the problem is his wife's emotional distance when, in reality, the problem is that he's dealing with unacknowledged depression. Or a client could intentionally hide the real problem because the client doesn't want to deal with it, doesn't want to talk about it. This usually happens because a person is ashamed or afraid that the therapist will judge or reject him or her. In these cases, people generally present a safer, more comfortable side of their difficulty to test the waters with a therapist and develop trust. You'll see this a lot with people who've been abused.

In both these cases, it's important to note, the presenting problem is still relevant. I mean, it's a "real" problem, too. It exists. It's aggravating. It needs to be addressed.

The difference is that it's usually part of a bigger problem and may even be a symptom of a deeper issue. When the real problem is addressed, usually the presenting problem resolves itself. Tackling the presenting problem head-on might not even be all that important to a client's ultimate recovery.

Maybe you've already guessed this, but the whole presenting problem versus real problem thing applies to more than just psychotherapy; it applies to the matter at hand—finding your dream job.

Allow me to illustrate. You probably picked up this book because you're ready for a change. You came to me for help and guidance because you believe that you'd be happier doing something else with your life and you want me to show you how to live out your dreams. In your mind, the problem is that you're not living the dream.

And you're right. That is the problem. But it's not why you need my help. And if I laid out the seven steps for you right now, it wouldn't make your problem go away. Because beneath this problem lies another problem—your real problem.

You.

Life Lesson Number Two: "You Are Your Own Worst Enemy"

You're not going to like this, but you probably already know it's true: In the quest to live the life you were made to live, you are your own worst enemy.

In your life, no one has caused more damage to your confidence, ruined more opportunities to take action, or sabotaged more good intentions than you have.

Have you ever seen those Demotivators posters from Despair, Inc.? They're spoofs of traditional motivational posters, and they're hilarious if you're in the right mood. If you're having a bad day, though, just skip 'em; go to YouTube and watch kitten videos instead. Seriously, some of the posters hit a little too close to home not to do some damage. Reading through the whole gallery at a low point in your life will send you to counseling for sure.

One of them has always stuck with me. "Dysfunction," it reads. "The only consistent feature in all your dissatisfying relationships is you."

Ouch. It stings because it's true. And it's true of more than just your relationships, right? I mean, think back to all your failures. What do they have in common? You.

I'm not trying to crush your spirits. I'm just being real with you. If you're ever going to stop settling and make the jump and find happiness living your dream, you're first going to have to face the enemy within. He or she is the real problem. And he or she is a doozy.

Hi, Dream Job! I'm Resistance

Remember life lesson number one? We were just talking about it: Settling is natural. And it probably took you all of eight seconds to realize that "shaking well" isn't. In fact, it's unreasonably, inexplicably hard.

By now you've realized it's not enough to recognize that settling is natural and that knowing you ought to shake well doesn't help. Even writing "shake well" reminders on Post-it Notes and plastering them all over your bathroom mirrors doesn't always do the trick. Most of the time you look at those notes and think to yourself . . . meh.

I have some good news for you: That push back, that weight you feel when you try to shake things up, isn't inexplicable. The bad news is that it never goes away.

Here's a fun fact: Virtually everything inside of you resists change. In the last chapter I briefly mentioned the biological principle of homeostasis, or the tendency to preserve a relatively stable equilibrium. In the body, these regulatory processes save your life every day. But there are other unconscious processes constantly at work in your heart and mind determined to maintain a different sort of homeostasis, one that isn't biologically necessary for survival. It might *feel* psychologically necessary for survival to maintain stability, but it's not.

One person who understood this well was the late teacher and writer George Leonard, who wrote a little book called *Mastery* in the early 1990s. In it, he writes about how homeostasis tries to prevent our body from making drastic changes and works to maintain stability in our lives—even if that stability is detrimental to us. Homeostasis, Leonard argues, is the main factor that stops people from changing their habits, especially if it's a sudden, dramatic change. You know, the kind of change pretty much all of us really want and try to achieve.

Another author, Steven Pressfield, writes at length about the same phenomenon, only he has a different word for it: "resistance."

I wrote about the phenomenon myself in my earlier book, *The Teen's Guide to World Domination*. That book explained a teen's world in terms of an ongoing battle against seven different "villains," like vampires and robots and zombies. What Leonard calls homeostasis and Pressfield calls resistance, I name "ghosts."

Ghosts are the most dangerous enemy and often the hardest to identify because they're in your head. They show up in the form of painful memories, past mistakes, hurtful words, and lies you've been told. Ghosts are the voice in your head that tells you that you'll never amount to anything, that you'll fail just like last time, that it's not worth trying, that it's okay to hit the snooze button one more time.

Ghosts don't want you to jump. In fact, they hate it when you even think about improving your life. Every time you set out to do something worthwhile, something you feel called to do, you can bet your bottom dollar you will meet with resistance—the ghostly whispers in your head that discourage you from trying or that lull you into complacency.

All of a sudden, you'll be flooded with self-doubt and regrets from recalled mistakes and missed opportunities. Trivial things will begin to preoccupy you. Old wounds will reopen. Your deepest fears will rise to the surface to cripple your intentions.

Ghosts are lingering, lurking liars, and, unfortunately, you can't escape them. You can't block them out because they're immaterial. They run through walls.

Issues you've suppressed and never fully dealt with will paralyze you and attempt to derail your dream before you ever get off the ground.

> You're afraid of being defective.
> You're afraid of being unworthy.
> You're afraid of being worthless.
> You're afraid of being insignificant.
> You're afraid of being incompetent.
> You're afraid of being alone.
> You're afraid of being hurt.
> You're afraid of being controlled.
> You're afraid of being disconnected.

You're afraid. We're all afraid of something.

Where do these ghosts come from? How did the enemy within even get here in the first place? I think part of the battle is recognizing that the enemy within is a force of nature. It's homeostasis. It's gravity. Inertia. It isn't personal at all. It affects everybody.

But resistance, on the other hand, is deeply personal. It affects everybody differently. It studies your Y factor and uses your

innermost fears and insecurities and even your strengths against
you. The enemy within is an expert at espionage and always
plays dirty. He'll echo the lies others told you: that you're not
smart enough, that you're not pretty, that you'll never amount to
anything.

The enemy within stockpiles ammo whenever you suffer injury and feeds off bitterness and fear. I spent a good portion of
my younger years tossing clips to the enemy within until its arse-
nal absolutely bristled with weapons to use against me. I couldn't
even take a shower without taking hits, but things were especially bad whenever I tried to get close to people. I was weakest
there. Growing up without my biological family, I had a lot of
trust issues and struggled with feeling unwanted and unloved. I
didn't believe I had value. So anytime I thought about opening
up to my foster parents, say, or wanted to ask out a girl, the enemy within would attack with devastating ambush. I'd usually
sabotage myself.

Your Real Problem Is That You're Whipped

The enemy within has you beaten. You haven't made the jump
because every time you get within sniffing distance, a sniper shot
takes you out.

You're a slave to fear.

You cannot ignore this. Changing your career without con-
fronting your ghosts is futile, exhausting, and potentially disas-
trous. Ghosts are pretty tough to ignore. They'll chase you as
long as you'll run. But, sort of like the ghosts in Super Mario,
when you face them, they stop chasing you. If you don't turn
around and deal with ghosts now, they're going to deal with you
over and over again.

So long as you aspire to do something good, something meaningful, something difficult and worth it, the enemy within will rise to block your path.

You can count on the fact that the enemy within is remarkably predictable. If you plan to jump, anticipate an ongoing confrontation with your inner demons. Step offtrack and abandon your goals and things will return to normal. Your heart might languish and die, but the enemy will leave you alone. The moment you admit defeat, you are allowed to go freely . . . back into bondage.

But the enemy can be overcome.

> **Reflection—Caton Vance** *Caton Vance wants to become a writer. He wrote and self-published his first book, but he's debating taking the next steps.*

I'm currently a twenty-five-year-old college grad working in a job that is completely unsatisfying. I am an account manager for a third-party administrator in health benefits. It's not a bad job. It's what I was told was the end goal when I was younger—the nine to five with a house and family. I mean, I'm there practically (just need the family), but I'm definitely not doing what I love. I'm doing what I thought I was supposed to do when someone is planning on getting married. Get the responsible job, the risk-free job, the one with the steady income and the insurance "just in case."

I'm at an interesting spot because most of what I love to do I have done a little of in some capacity, but never for money or any length of time. I wrote a book this past year and it was published through a couple of close friends of mine. It was the most rewarding thing I've done—creatively and spiritually, and I even made a little bit of money that I was able to buy my first piece of art with.

My situation hasn't changed much since writing the book. I had dreams of it selling out (which it did), but now we need to print more, start the process over again, and try other routes. I've also been advised it could be better—the book, that is—and it's true; it can be better. But I have this job that supplies me with all the day-to-day stuff I need. Money. This job allows me to live the life I've wanted to live since I became an adult. I can go out during the week, see my friends and family on the weekends. I get to party like a rock star and not be broke when the sun comes up. I can pay my bills, afford to buy new clothes. I can take care of myself. I've never fully been able to do that until this job. But when I wake up on Monday morning and I think about the week ahead, there's no excitement. No passion. There's no hopefulness in what I'm going to be doing.

My dream is to become a writer . . . a novelist . . . an essayist . . . a publisher . . . a speaker. Truly, I just want to be an effective communicator, someone who can communicate to those around that they are loved, that they have a purpose, that wherever they are at, they are totally okay. No matter what has happened, it can get better.

What's holding me back is that I do truly love my life—I live like a king. I know how lucky and blessed I am to be where I'm at in life. Part of what makes it so hard for me to jump is that I have some sort of complex that tells me maybe enough is enough. It could be some kind of ghost or resistance, but I have so much more than I ever imagined when I was younger. I grew up really poor and I'm part of a huge family. We had the bare essentials, but I showed up to my first basketball practice in fifth grade wearing jeans and cowboy boots because that's all I had to wear. I do want more, though. I do, yet I'm not sure if it's a selfish desire.

I believe things could be better and I could work in the realm of books. I also would like to work in the creative fields. I think I was built for it. I thrive when I'm with a group of people and there is newness and purpose, ideas and life. I get juiced up and excited to wake up and go to work. I've worked with a couple of designers and creatives over the years in various facets, and those were some of the most rewarding work hours I've ever experienced. But somehow I'm working in an office downtown in a job that is totally not who I am. I got the job because a year and a half ago I was in a relationship that was headed toward the altar and I was trying to do the right thing and get a "real" job. Well, now the relationship is over and I have my real job. But I don't want it anymore. I want to write a novel that will rock the *New York Times* bestseller list. I want to write a book that will change lives for the better. I want to tell a story that is more powerful than all the lies we live in.

I have many forms of resistance, and most of them are actually really great. I have a lot of friends (it's not bragging, it's just true), and I can't really go to any coffee shop and expect to work for a couple of hours without being interrupted. I have a large family that is always doing something, and

I feel a deep obligation to be part of everything my family does. I have a lot of interests, from fashion to wine to whiskey to adventures to skateboarding to reading. I let little things get in the way of writing all the time. New relationships and old pop up whenever there is time to finally sit in front of my notebook. It's hard for me to say no, and that might be the biggest form of resistance. I don't want to miss out on what is going on around me; I don't want to let people down when I don't show up to something I've been invited to. I want to be a part of everything, but I am waking up to the fact that I'm only one guy, and I don't have forever to do the things I desire. I'm only here for a moment, then gone like the grass at the end of summer.

Life Lesson Number Three: You Choose Your Own Adventure

There are a thousand ways to make a wrong decision, but there are also a thousand ways to make a right decision.

—STELLAN SKARSGÅRD

Want to beat the enemy within? Want to shake things up and overcome your natural tendency to settle, silence ghosts, and punch resistance in the face? Good. You'll have to if you ever hope to jump.

We've already established that this enemy within doesn't go down easy, so how do you beat it? I'll give you a clue: Remember our Jump GPS? Pull that back out for a sec and study your X factor—where you are right now.

You're standing on the edge of a choice.

Life Lesson Number Three: "You Choose Your Own Adventure"
Overcoming our natural tendency to settle isn't as easy as it sounds. Shaking is unnatural. It takes effort, and it requires risk.

As a kid, you had very few opportunities to steer your own life. You didn't get to make yourself sick eating cookies, jump off roofs onto mattresses, or stay up 'til 3:00 A.M. no matter how well your six-year-old self laid out your case. So if you were anything like me, you cherished the few instances where all the decisions were entirely up to you.

For me, I found this rush of freedom and control in the nostalgic, famous Choose Your Own Adventure books.

Do you remember those? One of them landed me—the reader—in a land of abominable snowmen. Another one set me down right in the middle of a nuclear meltdown. And there I was, eleven years old with the fate of the world in my hands.

I remember sitting underneath my covers with a flashlight and devouring these books. There must've been fifty of them, capable of thrusting heroism and bravery and genius on the average middle school student in just one or two sittings.

Thinking back on the reasons I (and maybe you) loved these books as a kid, I realized it was because they gave me a mental field trip away from the life I'd settled into. Every book whisked the reader away to a new world, but it was more than just a fantastical tour of a new setting.

There were options.

My choices made a difference.

In a world dominated by our teachers, parents, and people who meet the minimum height requirement to ride the adult rides, it gave us, and only us, an opportunity to choose. We got to choose whether or not to light the hibernating bear on fire or to attempt to inject the vampire with the serum even at the risk that he'd suck our blood.

And the books were relatively worry-free. These books gave us an opportunity to risk with little to no overanalysis. Worst-case scenario? When you turned to page 173, you died. You're lying there in the snow staring up at the sky waiting to be eaten by the ferocious abominable snowman, and you know what? Zero regret sweeps over you.

Oh, well. Flip back and choose a different path. No harm done. You're still safe in your bed.

Life Is an Adventure

Like the Choose Your Own Adventure books of childhood, your life is full of choices. Unlike these childhood stories, however, the stakes feel a little higher. There are real-world consequences here. If an abominable snowman eats you in real life, you don't get to flip back and choose a different path. (You would, however, probably get a Discovery Channel special made about you, so that's something.)

Sometimes your options feel overwhelming and the world seems like a giant multiple-choice test with no right answers. Try not to have a panic attack. The war between the ordinary and the extraordinary is waged on the x-axis, on tiny battlefields, in everyday routine decisions. One at a time.

Usually the choice can be simplified into two basic options:

Option A	Option B
Do this.	Do that.
Get out of bed.	Hit the snooze button.
Go to the gym.	Watch another episode.
Open the file and get to work.	Open Facebook.

These tiny decisions define where your life is heading and ultimately reinforce or hijack who you want to be.

Granted, there's nothing wrong with skipping the gym one day a week to watch another episode. A little rest can be healthy. But if you're calling in sick to eat Cheetos on a beanbag chair six days in a row, your life may not be headed toward the kind of greatness you're after.

When you think about it, options are synonymous with freedom. What is crazy is that, although we have opportunities to choose, we often choose not to. But that's what the enemy within tries to get us to do: Settle for indecision. Or bad decisions. Anything but forward motion.

We make small, incremental decisions that add up over time, that gradually form our habits and eventually shape a life that may or may not include anything that feels the least bit adventurous.

Then we wonder how we ended up here. Easy answer? We chose it, one step at a time, often like a crazy person, doing the same thing over and over again and expecting different results. It's silly to expect to arrive at a different destination if we never turn around to walk toward it.

Of course, "Life Is an Adventure!" is easy to say to a kid, for whom the world seems full of possibilities. But in adulthood, it becomes clear that choosing your adventure is harder to execute than it sounds. In my experience, most people don't see life as an actual adventure.

When I was in school, nobody felt as if we were in the middle of an adventure. We were all just trying to survive, to not be the kid whose eyes got scratched out of the yearbook photo or whose awkward build got analyzed and annotated on the bathroom wall. In fact, my story didn't at all live up to the kind of heroic sagas I would've deemed "adventurous." It was more along the lines of a modern Greek tragedy.

You'll get hung up on this if you don't realize that life is not *exactly* like a Choose Your Own Adventure book. But you probably already knew that.

I Didn't Choose This

As a kid, my life may have been an adventure, but I sure as hell didn't choose it. Not even a drunken idiot at gunpoint would choose the sort of "adventure" I had as a child.

In order to understand why I'm so appreciative of the opportunity to choose my own adventure as an adult, let me let you in on a little bit more about my childhood.

The word "choose" was practically foreign to me as a child, because I didn't really have any chances to make decisions for myself, let alone create my own adventures.

My life begins with a birth certificate declaring that I was "Josh Shipp—Orphan of the State." Why? Because immediately after I was born, my mother left me at the hospital. Not the first line of most fairy tales, huh?

Over the years, I was everyone's favorite hot potato, passed through foster care homes, moving nearly fifteen times in fifteen years. This meant, of course, that my world consisted of unfamiliar places, insecurity, and an eerie connection to the ghosts of previous foster children, whose toys and clothes I inherited. I remember, even at a young age, being acutely aware I was less of a person and more of a number, an adolescent statistic on a government list a social worker was assigned to check in on. Sometimes I was also just a paycheck for my foster parents.

This didn't seem like an adventure. Maybe, if you're into Disney- or Cinderella-style buildups, you could construe all this as pretransformation setup: the hardship that one day magically melts away into a land of loving parents, unending supplies of video games, and unshakeable confidence. But my adventure, in which I had no choice, didn't go that direction.

When I was eight years old, I was placed in a home with a bunch of boys of varying ages, all packed into the same room outfitted with bunk beds. There was no privacy or personal space, especially on the days one particular older boy would come and visit our room. Significantly bigger and more intimidating than any of us, he would sneak in and begin raping every one of his "foster brothers"—including me.

So again, I point out the obvious: This was definitely not the page I would have turned to if I were choosing my own adventure.

I know that this story—and my emotions while growing up in it—is anchored in heavy emotions. Loneliness. Isolation. Depression. You probably feel a sinking horror in your gut when you hear it. No one would wish this upon anyone, even their worst enemies. I certainly didn't choose this for myself.

But I Still Had Choices

Eventually, as I grew older, I had a bit more freedom. If I could sum up my teenage years in a scene from a movie, it would be a scene from an old Marlon Brando film called *The Wild One*. Marlon, who plays Johnny, rides around on his motorcycle and takes out his frustration on the world around him. At one point at a local dance, a girl asks what the letters "B.R.M.C." stand for on the back of their motorcycle jackets. "Black Rebels Motorcycle Club," he says. She turns to Johnny and asks, "What are you rebelling against, Johnny?" So he cocks his head as he turns to look at her, with an attitude only Marlon Brando can pull off. He looks into her eyes and replies, *"Whaddya got?"*

That was me.

I hated what life had dispensed to me, and, as a result, I wanted to rebel against anything and everything that came near me. If there was a rule, I wanted to break it. If there was a right way, I wanted the wrong way. This was the only thing that gave me a sense of power and control over those around me. Given the choice between conformity and nonconformity, I chose the latter. Given the choice between obedience and disobedience, same story. Given the choice between pleasing other people and pissing them off, well, let's just say I didn't make many friends. Rebellion was my choice.

I opted, for example, to act so horribly to several sets of foster parents that they had to report me and move me into different homes. I became so arrogant in my play for control that I clearly recall myself walking into a new home and smugly announcing to the other boys, "Watch this. I'll be kicked out of this house in two weeks." Several manipulative choices later, I'd engineered my exit, right on schedule.

I chose self-sabotage.

As things continued to get worse in this vicious cycle of bad leading to worse, I started to deal with my wild emotions by turning to food. Eating junk food was my drug of choice, and I fully indulged. Of course, I was soon being labeled as "the pudgy kid." (As if I didn't have enough labels already!) And, as you can imagine, fattening up in a world where the juvenile social scene treated obese kids like social lepers did not improve my adventure.

I would come home looking for ways to cope, and the only thing I could find was (you guessed it) more junk food.

Eventually, I came to a place in life where I was so depressed, so lonely, so empty that I tried to kill myself. Luckily, my desperate attempt was thwarted, but even that didn't deter me from my path of destruction. Before I knew it, I was doing time in jail for check fraud and nursing an extremely serious gambling problem. I can just picture the enemy within leaning back in his chair, linking his hands behind his head, and sighing in joyful contentment.

Fact: 50 percent of foster kids end up in jail, dead, or homeless. And that is exactly where I was headed.

I was severely limited by my inability to see that there was always more than one choice available. In every case, there were two. For every option A, there was an option B.

I couldn't get close to seeing two options, though, because I couldn't identify the larger tension inside of me. I thought my tensions were with everyone who had done me wrong—teachers, foster parents, and the system. But really I was missing a larger principle. The presenting problem was distracting me from the real problem: me. The enemy within.

It's always someone else's fault. It's our bosses' fault. It's the ridiculous way the company is organized. It's that nosey neighbor, that overbearing relative, that girlfriend or boyfriend who makes daily attempts to ruin your life.

When we believe we're the victim and it's us against them, it's natural to adopt a constant attitude of defiance.

Too often, though, my guess is that we are still often misidentifying the tension. This misdirected tension is like a spiral staircase that descends, one flight at a time, into the abyss. Something bad happens, and we react by moving one step lower. New scenario, new response. One step lower.

The fact is that it takes more effort to walk up, especially if you've already made a lot of "progress" down. Settling is natural, after all.

Once we identify the enemy within, however, option B opens up. Suddenly, we notice there is another way. Sure, the stairs go down. But, as it turns out, they also go up.

This is the lesson of my adolescence and something I've come back to again and again in my adulthood. We move two steps up, but it doesn't mean life automatically becomes a fairy tale. We have to keep noticing our options, keep choosing the good ones over the bad ones, the best ones over the just normal ones.

You see . . .

Even Little Choices Can Make a Huge Difference

Sometimes we forget this.

I was doing research on food items and their respective levels of water content once because I thought that eating things with high water content would be good for me. My research was going pretty well for a while, until, inevitably, I got sidetracked and things got weird. Forty minutes later, I found myself searching for "water content of a baby," "water content of Josh Shipp," "water content of Google," "water content of water," "water content of Keith Richards," and so on. Believe me, it was a downward spiral.

Eventually, I snapped out of it and landed on a site that was much more practical. It spelled out the water content of bananas, potatoes, shampoo, pee, clouds, and blood. Cool. But I was dumbfounded when I came to the entry about watermelon, because the percentage was shockingly high—like 94-percent-water kind of high. I mean, clouds have high water content—97 percent—but who's surprised by that? But watermelons?

Is it just me, or does that seem impossible?

What really blew me away was what this meant about the difference between the makeup of a watermelon and a cloud. Picture a bright billowy cloud in the sky. Got it? Then picture a watermelon. What these studies were claiming is that there is only a 3 percent difference between the makeup of a cloud and one of those oblong stripey green fruits you eat in the summer (and/or blow up on the Fourth of July).

If you're a chemist or biologist or geneticist, this might not be impressive to you at all. Maybe this little illustration sounds unsophisticated; you could think of a dozen better examples of small differences yielding massively different results without even trying. Okay, perfect. Do that.

My point remains the same.

What's true in chemistry and genetics is true of our choices: It often only takes a small shift, a tiny change, to make a huge difference in who and what we become. You *can* avoid settling for an ordinary, unfulfilling life by making a series of small changes.

Choose Adventure

You chose to pick up this book because, deep down, you probably still have the hunger of an adolescent who—at some level—wants to choose your own adventure. I know that hunger is a big part of why I'm writing it. You want to practice that specific career that makes you feel alive, to build relationships that give you butterflies in your stomach, to take on aspirations that excite you to wake up to your alarm clock every day.

I can officially say that I am now living an amazing adventure. But it didn't just happen to me. I had to get intentional and go out and choose it. Now, I've reaped so many benefits from choosing to shake things up and making intentional decisions to overcome the enemy within that adventure has almost become my default. Whenever the opportunity presents itself, I have vowed to myself that I will choose adventure. Life is too short to start settling.

When assessing your life, it's important to remember to "shake well." That's the first step in remembering that success comes to those who are ready to start looking for it. The next step is to choose your own adventure, by shaking in the right direction.

A desire for adventure is still alive in you. Don't suppress it.

As you get older, you will realize that comfort and familiarity often become the enemies of adventure. It's hard to dream when you don't want to sacrifice the house your mortgage binds you to or your two weeks of paid vacation. If you're not careful, you'll find yourself saying, "This isn't my perfect job, but it's good enough."

Listen to me closely. "Good enough" is a death sentence for anyone who has been called to an adventure. "Good enough" is a drug that keeps you just sedated enough to forget the passion you once had. The drug of "good enough" will keep you locked in your silent prison forever, as you experience the agony of a story never told.

So here you are, an adult with a history of the choices you've made, both the good ones and the bad. You are starting to see your future, your dream job, but you must realize that it's not going to happen unless you start shaking things up and taking small steps in the right direction.

It's safe to assume there will be no parades in your honor for shaking up your life in these small 3-percent-type ways, but remember: consciously choosing to make these little decisions can dramatically change your end result.

NOW is the only moment that you have complete control over; the x-axis is the only one you can actively, directly influence. You can't change the past and you can't guarantee the future, but how you treat this very moment will affect how the past is remembered and create the options you have tomorrow.

What you do right *now* is the most important decision you can make. This is your adventure. Choose wisely.

Reflection—Heather Colletto *"One year ago, if you could have pictured yourself anywhere today, where would it have been?" My husband asked me this on my twenty-fourth birthday, which we were celebrating at our new home in rural northern Thailand. Surrounded by mountains and lush rice fields in our little wooden house, I knew my answer immediately: "Right here."*

The answer wasn't just living in Thailand, but being a part of what we were doing there. We had just officially come on board as the communications team for a young and growing nonprofit, The SOLD Project, fighting on the prevention side of child exploitation. On my twenty-third birthday, the dream would have been nearly unthinkable: living in Thailand and working in the midst of this exciting new nonprofit. And yet there I was, twenty-four years old to boot.

I had learned about the SOLD Project just over a year before, when I was researching ways to get involved in the fight against human trafficking. As a writer without social work or law under my belt, I wasn't sure there was a place for me in this issue. But SOLD was an organization for young artists, and I was accepted into their internship program. I began participating in their stateside work as much as possible, raising awareness and sponsoring an at-risk student so she could stay in school and avoid work in red-light districts. Our investment in the organization and its mission grew, and, after participating in an invite-only exposure trip to Thailand with SOLD, we decided to move there as full-time staff. SOLD couldn't afford to pay us, but we could fund-raise and live off the generous support of family and friends.

Professionally, the jobs were a huge leap forward. Personally, the opportunity was impossible to pass up. We sold what we could, shoved our belongings into a five-by-ten storage unit, gave away our car, sent our cat to my parents' house, and hit the road to raise funds and awareness for the org and, more specifically, our new jobs. We drove from Grand Rapids to Los Angeles to Minneapolis to Philadelphia, sleeping on friends' couches and hosting fund-raising events.

After three months on the road, we finally moved to Chiang Rai, Thailand, to tell the stories of at-risk kids from the village where we lived. We wrote blogs, managed social media, connected students with sponsors, and served as on-the-ground representatives of this prevention work that was—and still is—changing a village where more than half the kids once dropped out of school to go work in the cities.

We took a huge risk in the move, dipping into savings and quitting jobs, but here we were, celebrating the dream on my twenty-fourth birthday. We were working jobs we were good at with an organization we were passionate about, on this exciting and exotic adventure we'd never forget. I felt sorry for our friends who were buying houses and having babies and working office jobs. I was doing something that mattered. They seemed to be just trying to pay the bills.

I felt that way each day when the kids rode their bikes from school to the Resource Center, where we lived. We taught English, played games, exchanged Thai and English words, showed them love and, hopefully, that they had immeasurable value. We offered whatever skills we could that would give these kids a fighting chance. SOLD grew into several English classes each week, a computer lab, and human-trafficking-awareness courses for the community. With the help of local staff that we came to know and love, the village was changing. The future of these kids was changing.

Every afternoon, we hugged the kids tightly, lost a game of badminton soundly, laughed over the language barrier, and waved good-bye as they rang their bicycle bells all the way down the dirt road to their homes, where parents would just be arriving from a day in the fields. I'd hop on a motorbike to grab fresh vegetables and meat from the market. We mastered the art of Thai curry while the sun set behind the mountains, which grew the coffee beans we'd grind and drink in the morning.

But I spent a lot of those mornings with a French press, deeply unsatisfied.

That dissatisfaction led to guilt. If I'm in this dream scenario, why am I not fully content? What am I doing wrong? It wasn't, "Oh, maybe this isn't my dream after all." It was, "Crap, this *is* my dream, and it's not as fulfilling as I thought it would be." I worked harder and harder to appreciate every moment and relish the opportunity. But a lot of days really sucked. We were away for a loss in my family, hurtful miscommunications arose within the team, and we often felt lonely beyond words. I grew jealous of my friends back home who were in their homes, surrounded by family, and starting their own little families. And, no, the irony was not lost on me.

Then we hit a big bump in the journey. Sort of literally. A few months of bumpy rural roads on a motorbike led me to a severe spinal-disc herniation that caused excruciating pain and complete loss of feeling in my right leg. We traveled eight hours by ambulance for an MRI that revealed I needed spine surgery—and fast. We traveled another twelve hours to a hospital for surgery. We had insurance, but they played dirty and wouldn't pay, claiming my (otherwise healthy) spine was deteriorating and the injury qualified as the infamously noncovered "preexisting condition." The weeks of hospital stay and surgery went on our emergency credit card. We'd never carried credit card debt in our lives, and suddenly we were sinking fast under the monthly bills and high interest from the hospital stay and spine surgery. Broke and getting broker, we had no choice but to return to the United States after only six months in Thailand. We returned to no car and no job and no home and no cat.

My husband continued working from the States for SOLD as director of communications while I looked for full-time employment that would help dig us out of our growing debt and get us better health insurance. We lived in Philadelphia with my sister's family, spending six months in their hospitality and my little niece's pink bedroom. We drove a car borrowed from my parents, the one I learned to drive in when I was sixteen. We looked for housing, but the move and the surgery had gutted our savings, and we couldn't afford living near the big city. We had a lawyer friend threaten to sue the insurance company on our behalf, and they immediately cut us a check, but it was too little, too late.

I had enjoyed a dream job for such a short time, and now I couldn't even get an interview. I probably should have picked up a job at Starbucks or something, but I was certain that I could return to important world-changey nonprofit work just as soon as a very important nonprofity person who was hiring received this forty-third cover letter and résumé. The interviews never came. We eventually moved out of my sister's house and into a Midwest city with a lower cost of living and a random job opportunity that I only took after disappointed tears and a lot of pride swallowing. I became an admissions counselor at a university, which is a role often filled by recently graduated college students.

I arrive at work Monday through Friday and sit (well, stand, actually—it's better for my back) at my desk from 8:00 a.m. to 5:00 p.m. I do not watch the rice farmers harvest their grains while I sip my morning coffee. I do not see the smiling faces of at-risk children every afternoon. I do not speak proudly when I tell strangers at parties what I do for a living. I am not doing something that matters. I am just trying to pay the bills.

I don't know what my next dream is. Sometimes my dream is a house and a baby, but I feel like I'm betraying my younger (judgmental) Thailand-bound self. Sometimes my dream is another overseas adventure, but we need health insurance that covers physical therapy. Right now, my dream is to be in a nonprofit again that makes me feel like I'm really, truly contributing to the greater good. In the meantime, I have to deal with this terrible realization that I *like* my job as an admissions counselor. As in, I like going to work every day, and I have fun while I'm there. It has literally taken a ridiculous amount of time to be able to confess that. It's not deeply soul satisfying or anything, but neither was my dream job in Thailand. Which makes me suspicious that *no* job is going to be that satisfying, and it might be more of a heart issue than a job issue. For now, my heart is happy and satisfied enough. Now that we have a salary and steady health insurance (even dental! *dental!*), we have space in our budget to support people going to do those exciting world-changey nonprofit things all over the world. Kind of like those people who supported us when we went to Thailand. Our support checks, thanks to my admissions counselor job, can be generous and sent with love and respect and only the smallest side of jealousy.

I'm still working through what the lessons are here. Maybe we "failed," but it wasn't a waste of time. We're still deeply invested in the SOLD Project. We gained valuable professional experience. We had a once-in-a-lifetime opportunity to get to know the lovely people of this village in northern Thailand. We see that you can make a difference for the greater good even in an office job. (I know, right?) I know that no job will ever satisfy, so I can skip all that "if only . . ." stuff for now.

We "failed" for reasons that were primarily outside of our control. It sucked. But we survived. And, just like our mama taught us, we're better people for it.

Life Lesson Number Four: You Can Only Control Yourself

We're getting close to those steps I've promised you. But there's a final lesson to impart. You see, I've chosen to describe life as an adventure for a reason: You don't know how it will end.

Adventures, by definition, are unusual and exciting and typically hazardous; adventure always involves risk and uncertainty. The sooner you're able to accept this, the sooner you'll be ready to jump.

Overcoming the enemy within requires a conscious choice to do the hard thing. And it's risky, which is always frightening because it brings us face-to-face with an uncomfortable reality: You don't have control of the outcome. When you shake, you never know how things will turn out. That's scary. There's a chance that shaking things up will not only be hard but also end very, very poorly.

There's a great moment in Martin Scorsese's film *Hugo*, where the lead character, an orphan boy named Hugo who lives inside the walls of a Paris train station, leads his new friend Isabelle somewhere they both know isn't safe. Isabelle, who earlier in the film admits that she's never had an adventure before, warns,

"We could get into trouble!" Without missing a beat, Hugo replies: "That's how you know it's an adventure."

Unlike the Choose Your Own Adventure books of childhood, it's not as simple as just flipping to page 89 and then restarting if you don't like the outcome of your choices. In fact, the bigger the adventure you chase, the larger the list of things you can't control will grow. That's what happens when you step out into the world with the intent to do something that matters: The enemy within raises up to remind you that you could "get into trouble." You could fail. Things could go very, very badly.

You could choose poorly.

Choice can be paralyzing. Choices remind us that we can't have it all, that "all of the above" isn't usually an option outside multiple-choice tests.

We're afraid of risk. We're afraid of regret. We're afraid to choose, mourning the loss of the choices we'll lose.

If this sounds like the worst news ever, it isn't. In fact, few things in life are more freeing than acknowledging and accepting that virtually everything in the entire world is beyond your control.

Think about it. If you can't control it, it's completely pointless to worry. You pull the teeth out of fear.

In our most sane moments, it's easy to accept the premise that life should be shaken well. The problem, of course, is that life is rarely sane. A lot of the time, daily life feels rushed and crammed with to-do lists. It may venture off the sitcom-perfect script you had penned in your imagination. You begin to panic and protect yourself, reacting to outside forces and simply scrambling to keep your head above water. In those desperate moments, settling actually sounds kind of nice.

The routines you call life aren't flagrantly disappointing or destructive. The wind has just slowly, inch by inch, blown your ship into calm waters in a safe harbor of someone else's choosing. Maybe life is boring, uneventful, the same yesterday as it was the day before and the day before. It's nice enough, really. And, even though it's not for you, you settle for good enough. It might not be an adventure, but at least you feel safe. You feel like you have control.

The (Futile) Pursuit of Control

The issues of choice and control are inextricably linked. While we celebrate options and freedom of choice, we're terrified of losing control. Most of the choices we make in life are motivated by a desire to achieve or maintain control of our present circumstances and future life. We hate uncertainty, which is ironic, since uncertainty is a byproduct of freedom. We want to have our cake and eat it, too.

A huge part of the appeal for me of the Choose Your Own Adventure books of childhood, formulaic as they were, was that they offered me something I was desperately missing in my life: control.

As a foster kid, I didn't have any say in where I lived, who I lived with, or how long I would stay. And I never felt less control than when I was abused and believed I had no one to run to for help. Unless I was reading those books, I literally had no control over myself or the world around me. I hated that.

During my teenage years, it was a pursuit of control that fueled my rebellion. Your story may be different. There are two ways people typically try to exercise control: by obeying or by rebelling.

As I mentioned, I was one of the rebels. The rebellious ones don't trust the system at all and figure they're better off on their own doing their own thing. They break the rules to feel powerful and to assert themselves. Usually, rebels end up hurting themselves.

The obedient ones try to work within the system. They figure that if they can just play by the rules, they can ensure a happy life for themselves. It's like a subconscious belief in karma: Good things happen to good people. Except, obviously, sometimes they don't.

Life loves throwing wrenches into our plans to remind us that we're only human.

You don't get a chance to choose every adventure. Sometimes adventures just come and find you and mess up all your plans. You get laid off, left at the altar, betrayed by a friend. A storm or a stock market crash levels your savings. Freak accidents and unexpected diagnoses change everything in an instant.

As a kid, you think you'll have more control when you're bigger, older, and grown-up . . . but you don't. You have more choices as an adult, but no more control. Not really. So we make lame choices because we're scared, hoping that safe choices will keep us safe and ensure our happiness. We avoid risk, stifle our dreams, and settle into a life we never wanted—all because we were afraid of ending up in a life we never wanted.

The enemy within deserves a high five and a medal for that strategy, because it works almost every time.

To conquer our inner freak-outs and disarm the enemy within, we have to learn an important lesson.

Life Lesson Number Four: "You Can Only Control Yourself"
I remember that in one of my foster homes a little sign hung in the kitchen with a well-known prayer on it:

> *Lord, grant me the serenity to accept the things I cannot change, the courage to change the things I can, and the wisdom to know the difference.*

I had no idea what it meant at the time. In fact, I remember looking at it and trying to decipher it, but words like "serenity" might as well be written in hieroglyphics for a fifth grader. And even if I had understood its literal meaning, I wasn't ready to apply its wisdom.

As an adult, though, those words register in the deepest parts of me. They not only summon me to celebrate my freedom to choose adventure but also inspire me to invite others to bask in theirs as well.

When we become paralyzed by indecision out of fear, the tension comes from misunderstanding what we can and can't control.

Guess what you can't control?

Here's the short list:

- What has happened or will happen to you
- What other people think, say, or do
- What you've already done
- The length of your own or anyone else's life

This list could go on forever, probably literally. The universe is a vast, vast place, and you exercise measurable influence on just the tiniest part of it: you.

And you don't even control most things related to you, even really basic things like your safety. In fact, there's pretty much just one thing you can control, and that is your decisions—what you choose to do.

Life Happens

I have young friends who were killed in car accidents. I've known newly married couples with a perfect life ahead of them who lost a baby because of unforeseen issues just hours after she was born.

I have a friend who was twenty-seven years old when he learned he had an inoperable cancerous brain tumor and, to make matters worse, only a few years left to live. Think about his options. Option A is how most people respond; it's what the enemy within always encourages. He can misdirect his tension at the world, at the medical field that fails to provide an answer, at the people who fail to understand his unique circumstances, even at the god who made him. He can lash out at everything and everyone who fails to provide him with the life he wants. Of course, this option won't change anything, except possibly changing him into a bitter, angry person.

Thankfully, my friend realizes he has an option B. He gets that he can accept what he cannot change and pursue the best option available to him. He can channel his energy and emotion into building his immune system and fighting the cancer with everything he's got. And if you were to ask my friend with the brain tumor, he would tell you that cancer was a gift that forcefully pushed him out of his comfort zone. It confronts him every day and says, "Get busy living or get busy dying."

This is the way life works. Pain respects no person. If you are in this world long enough, disappointment and frustration will come to you. You will get fired. You will be broke. You will get mugged. You will lose friends. You will be falsely accused. You will be overlooked, unappreciated, and sometimes betrayed.

Bad things can and will happen to you. There simply are things that happen that you cannot control.

As you consider making the jump, it's important to understand all this. Reading this book—using the Jump GPS, facing your identity, learning not to settle, overcoming the enemy within, choosing your own adventure, and following the seven steps— will *not* guarantee success. Nothing will. If you're reading this book to "follow the rules" so that life smiles on you and leads you happily by the hand into the dream career you've always wanted without so much as a hiccup, you're going to be disappointed.

A GPS can tell you where you are and help you get from A to B, but it can't ensure a smooth ride. Eventually, you have to leave room for reality.

Sometimes, there's traffic. Sometimes a road is shut down. Sometimes you blow a tire, or a deer jumps into your lane, or a drunk driver runs you off the road. Sometimes there is an F-4 tornado standing between you and your destination. A GPS can't predict or prevent such things. It can point you in the right direction, but then life happens. You can't control it. But you can control what you do about it. You can wait patiently, take a detour, change the tire, brake, swerve, reroute, refuel, and keep going.

Alternatively, you can freak out, pull over, use your smartphone to sell your car on Craigslist, and sit down in the grass crying hot angry tears because things didn't go your way. You'll never reach your destination like that.

You can use hardship as a catalyst for shaking things up or let the enemy within use it to talk you into settling. You can choose to press on or back down.

This is a tough lesson. If you're buried in the scars of your past, unable to know the difference between what you can and cannot control, take a breather. Just relax. It's okay not to move forward just yet.

However, as you learn to "accept the things you cannot change," I hope you also learn to "change the things you can."

It's Time for You to Make a Decision

On my reality TV show *Jump Shipp,* at the end of each episode there is a moment where I have two silver briefcases sitting on the desk. The "jumpers" (a name we created for those going through the jump process) have been pushed to their limits. They've been challenged, stressed out, and thrown out of their comfort zones. At the end of the show, you can actually see the pain on their faces, knowing the decision they are about to make will change the course of their lives. But like I said, no one can do this on their own, so when they must choose, we surround them by their spouses, extended family members, and friends. All in all it comes down to *this* precise moment. A decision with only two options.

No jump or jump.

Decision Number One: In briefcase one, labeled, NO JUMP, I tell them I've placed $2,500 of my own cash (which is true). Not a bad thing to walk away with. A couple grand could make a dent in most people's financial worries. I do this because I want them to grapple with the appeal—the safety—of staying in their same old lives.

Decision Number Two: In the second briefcase, labeled JUMP, is something I can't tell them about. Why? Because that's life. You don't get to know the results of the decisions you make ahead of time. You can't predict the future. You have no guarantees. When you make a decision like this, you take a serious risk. But you also open yourself up to the rewards as well.

I'm proud, and even a little surprised, to say that after going through the seven-steps process on the show, none of the jumpers, not one, has selected the NO JUMP briefcase. And trust me, as we planned the show, we actually wanted a few people to choose the NO JUMP briefcase! We wanted to show the audience that some people just didn't have the guts. We didn't want their decisions to appear to be special "reality TV miracles," out of reach for ordinary folks like you and me. But they all chose to make this life-changing decision to jump.

It's always incredible to watch someone decide to accept uncertainty and take a risk to follow their dream. In that moment, they've learned to control the only thing they can: their decisions. They've decided to find themselves. They've decided not to settle. They've decided to face the enemy within, choose their own adventure, and take a risk. They've decided to JUMP.

So, what will it be? Are you going to let fear of what you can't control keep you from taking an active role in shaping your future? Or are you going to accept that uncertainty is inescapable and risk stepping into the adventure you know you were meant to live?

You're as ready as you'll ever be.

You can take the money and walk away.

Or you can JUMP.

Up to you.

> **Reflection—Jonathan Stoner** *Hi. My name's Jonathan. I turned thirty-one last July and work as a full-time documentary photographer, working mainly on weddings, engagements, and—what I really enjoy—photojournalism. In May 2011, I graduated with a degree in film studies. I actually attended college later in life, after spending a bit of time traveling and learning quite a few life lessons along the way. I had the opportunity to work for an organization called Youth with a Mission for nearly four years, spending quite a bit of time in Hawaii, Uganda, and Ireland—just to name a few places. While I worked for Youth with a Mission, I did everything from leadership training with college students to creating short films to acting as a coleader on several mission trips overseas.*

As I said before, I'm currently working as a freelance photographer full-time. This past October, I got married to the most amazing woman ever—and ever since, my wife and I have been dreaming, discussing, and plotting ways to get out to California. (This planned escape may or may not be helped by the fact that she's actually from the Golden State.) Ever since I can remember, I have loved film and every aspect of film production. It's more than a passion. It's an obsession.

One of the things I love the most about film is the ability to visually tell someone's story. I firmly believe that everyone, no matter who you are, has a story to tell. Inside each person is a story just waiting to be told—and I want to tell it. Maybe that's why my biggest passion in filmmaking is creating documentary films.

My lifelong dream has been to learn the ins and outs of the film business—

even if that means going back to school. There are days that I wake up feeling that anything is possible, like anything I want to do is attainable.

But there are other days, too. Days when I feel hesitant.

On days like those I feel fear. Fear of failure. Fear of making the wrong decision. Fear of just about everything. I worry that if I make the jump, I'll sink. On the other hand, I also fear that I've waited too long and that I'll never really end up doing what I feel made to do. The truth is: I'm scared.

I guess part of my fear is financial—digging myself deeper into debt or not being able to support my family. I'm fearful of not being able to find work in what I really want to do. I'm hesitant about actually getting out to California, beginning to chase my dream—and ending up falling on my face. What would I do then?

Above all, I fear not having what it takes to actually make it.

And so fear paralyzes me.

Maybe you know what that is like.

My saving grace is my wife. She is fearless, always pushing me to take risks when it comes to my dreams. If it wasn't for someone in my life who sees the big picture and pushes me to be everything I can be, I'm not quite sure where I'd be. I'm still on the journey—still dealing with my fears and doubts—but with her encouragement and belief in me, I'm beginning to take the steps necessary to live out my dream. I'm not there yet, but I'm on my way.

Maybe you're in the same boat as Jonathan—paralyzed by your fears and doubts. Don't let your fears and your doubts dictate who you are and what you can do. Your fears and your doubts do not define who you are—your passions, your talents, and your dreams do. Don't let fear paralyze you. Sure there are some unknowns, but once you take the first step, you'll see the path a little more clearly. Take another step and the fears and doubts that you feel begin to stop holding sway over your dream.

Because it's YOUR dream.

And it's time to take that first step.

A Prejump Warning . . .

The time has come to begin your jump! But wait . . . one more small thing.

One of my role models is author and talk show host Dave Ramsey. He's done amazing work for me and many others in the area of personal finance. And one of the reasons he has been so successful in leading people through life change is because he realized that people need small, manageable challenges that sustain the feeling that victory is attainable.

I want to echo this "baby step" theory to give you the small victories you need to Jump Ship. My plan, all said and done, ended up consisting of seven steps. Each of them is equally important. So it's key that you commit yourself to each of them equally if you really want to make your dream job a reality.

Before I unload the *Jump Ship* seven-step plan, I want to discuss why it's so important. The following random message is brought to you courtesy of my ADD.

I'm not a huge sci-fi fan. I respect it appropriately. But I must admit, I'm completely in love with *Battlestar Galactica*. If you haven't watched it, just try to do so without going underground for a month, losing your job, and forgetting to feed your children or your cat. They deserve better.

Why are we talking sci-fi? Well, there is a common element among *Battlestar Galactica, Star Wars, Star Trek, Doctor Who,* and just about every space-travel story. Each of these shows has references about traveling beyond "light speed." Viewers get the impression that anything that outpaces light speed is worth tuning in for.

For most of us, comprehending light speed seems just as difficult as surpassing it. I can imagine what one hundred miles per hour looks like. I may or may not have tried that in my car, depending on whether you are or are not my wife. I can even imagine what two hundred miles per hour looks like. I've seen films and images of planes as they break the sound barrier. I think I can even start to wrap my mind around Mach 1 or Mach 2. But I have to acknowledge the limits of my mind when it comes to envisioning the speed of light, which is 670,616,629 miles per hour.

Just under 671 million miles an hour. For all earthbound intents and purposes, that's pretty much instant. If you had a plane that could travel that fast, you could fly around the planet seven and a half times in a single second. That's insane. Out in space, however, where distances between planets and stars and solar systems are also beyond comprehension, even light speed turns out to seem pretty slow. Everything is so far apart. It would take more than four years for us to reach the nearest star.

But, since we really can't grasp what light speed looks like, our ignorance becomes a very helpful tool to screenwriters with plots based on traveling to the vast, unreached areas of space. Otherwise, sci-fi space travel could get pretty tedious pretty quickly. Everyone just accepts that these spaceships can cover huge distances really, really fast.

In *Star Wars,* Han Solo made it clear that the *Millennium Falcon* was the "fastest ship in the galaxy." And, with the help of special effects, you saw that speed in action. In *Star Trek,* Captain Kirk traveled at "warp speed," using what they called "warp drive."

In *Battlestar Galactica,* each of the ships "spools up the FTL drive" ("faster than light drive"), and then they "jump." (They actually say "jump" instead of "engage" or "punch it!" or "go" or "giddy up" or whatever.)

If you are going to jump, to move your career forward at an incredible rate, maybe even near the speed of light, be warned up front: This always involves taking on new risks.

This is why, whenever traveling at such speeds, sci-fi movies always highlight the importance of careful planning before jumping. And this may be the one instance where sci-fi principles hold true in real life. You have to plot the jump. No matter how critical you feel it is to jump right now, jumping without preparation is likely to end in ruin. Or, as Han rebuked an impatient and naive Luke Skywalker, "Traveling through hyperspace ain't like dusting crops, boy! Without precise calculations, we could fly right through a star or bounce too close to a supernova, and that'd end your trip real quick, wouldn't it?"

When we seek to live life with more power, to turn things up a notch, we have to plot our moves to the best of our abilities. We have to know where the resistance will come from. We have to know the resources available to us. We have to know our orientation: to understand where we've been, where we are, and where we want to go.

Most of the people I come into contact with *think* they're ready. This was true of my younger self as well. I thought I had it all figured out. So I wouldn't blame you if you were tempted to skip over the first few chapters because what you *really* want to do is start your jump. You want the fast track to step one.

But this illusion of overnight success, of rushing to a victory, often backfires. So before you start designing your logo, laying out your new venture's Web site, or printing your business cards, please join me in committing to plot our jumps. Make a conscious decision now to do your homework, to calculate your moves, so that you don't end up jumping into the middle of a black hole that, metaphorically speaking, has the potential to suck all the life out of your dream and crush your hopes.

I'm going to switch metaphors on you for a second, in case this whole light-speed thing isn't your style. Imagine for a minute that you're about to begin a long-distance cross-country race. Even if you've never run a minute in your life, you know that in these races there's always a starting line and a finish line—there's a point A and a point B—and the goal is to get from start to finish before everyone else. But in between, there's the trail.

Hear me on this: runners have to follow the trail. The trail might curve all over the place through the woods, across streams, up hills, and around obstacles, and it might not seem like the most direct route from point A to point B. But the runner who just cuts across the trail and jogs over the finish line without covering all the ground in between hasn't won the race. Similarly, a runner can't start the race halfway down the trail, skipping the whole beginning, and expect to win.

These seven steps are kind of like that, except instead of getting disqualified for cheating, you end up depressed because you're overwhelmed and confused and a little bit lost. Don't skip around. Don't skim over certain chapters because you feel like you're "past that." Read them all the way through and in the order they appear to get the big picture first. Then go back and reread whatever parts you feel you need to focus on. But the seven steps are in a specific order for a reason. That's the way the trail goes; that's the route from point A to point B.

I wrote this book because I've been down this path. With hard-earned experience and the guidance of others, I've drawn up the map. And you bought it. If you didn't plan on following it, that was a rather senseless purchase. Having a map in your glove box (or an app on your smartphone) isn't going to keep you from getting lost if you never look at it.

One last note about this whole race metaphor in case some of you leave with the wrong idea: Life—and jumping ship—isn't a race. You don't win by getting "there" (wherever that may be) faster than anyone else, and you don't lose if someone reaches their dream before you or earlier in life or whatever. How you compare to others isn't important. Neither is making a specific time or hitting specific deadlines. This is about you making the journey to where you're supposed to be. Speed is great, but determination and persistence are better. When you get there, if you haven't cut any corners, you've won.

If you'll remember at the beginning of the first section, "It's Time for a Change," I said there were a few lessons that took me a long time to learn for myself. On many occasions, I got lucky and stumbled into some truth. Or got not so lucky and got beaten over the head with it. In the end, though, things turned out all right, and I hope the wisdom I've gleaned from my experiences will help you avoid having to learn things the hard way.

As you move through your jump plan, if you feel stuck (and you will), revisit these lessons. They've always pushed me through to the next step, and they will push you through, too.

Along these lines, Josh Ritter, a phenomenal songwriter and singer, has a lyric that inspires me to pursue the best for my life. In a song called "California," he sings about a person moving out to California to search for the dream. You could imagine the naysayers telling him that he'll fail, that many people have gone before him and, yes, many people will come after him, but fortunately he can feel where *his* story should go. My favorite line is, "Don't say it's been done a hundred thousand times, because this one is mine."

Yes, it's a story, but it's *your* story. It's your epic story that is yet to be told. And according to Maya Angelou, there is nothing more agonizing that your untold story.

As you continue reading, embrace the idea that you are the entrepreneur of your life. The captain of your ship. You are venturing into the new world. You are a pioneer. You are an explorer. You are an astronaut. This story is yours. Own it.

Final checklist before jump . . .

Your pants are secure around your waist and—just like Bruce Dickinson—you plan to make gold records.

You have chosen *not* to accept settling but to shake and invite new unplanned moments into your life.

You are choosing to move beyond the ghosts of your past, to choose your own adventure, and to shake in the right direction.

You know your exact vocational location through your Jump GPS and understand how your past and present impact your future.

You are dedicated to sticking with the plan, which will do its best to keep you clear from disaster.

FTL drive is spooled up.

Boards are green.

3 . . . 2 . . . 1 . . .

Jump.

PART TWO: Making the Jump

Step One: Define Your Dream Job

> *If you limit your choices to what seems possible or reasonable, you disconnect yourself from what you truly want, and all that is left is compromise.*
>
> —ROBERT FRITZ

The only people who can change the world are people who want to. Changing the world is a primal calling. We were made to create, to do, to shape and reshape the world we live in and make it better—not simply to just take up space.

I hope that this doesn't come as a surprise, but you'll never land your dream job if you've never taken the time to define what your dream job actually is. Now that you've decided to shake things up and make the jump, the first step is figuring out what, exactly, you're jumping for.

DO THIS STEP OR ELSE

Only a fool jumps without first considering where he might land. The first step to making a successful jump and achieving your dream is having a dream to jump for. You can't refine an idea you haven't had. You can't plan to reach a goal you've never set. Until you have a dream to aim for, jumping won't take you anywhere but up—and down like a stone.

Before you actually jump, you must first learn to be a dreamer. Remember the Jump GPS? Steps one and two are all about solving for Z. In the first part of this book, we took a hard look at X and Y—hopefully you have a good handle of where you are and where you've been. Now, we're going to use that same formula to figure out the Z, where you want to go.

There are at least two phases of defining any dream. The first is the no-holds-barred magical world, where everything is possible, there are no restrictions, the constraints of reality fly out the window, and wishful thinking is highly encouraged. The second phase of defining a dream is a reality check, when you take your dream and treat it practically, considering all the possible obstacles and requirements needed. We will get to that second phase in step two. But the heart of step one requires you to set aside all those practical concerns, counterarguments, and "yeah, buts" for a healthy space of time and just let your imagination go wild.

It is very important to start dreaming without any restrictions. When you settle on something you really feel good about, we'll move to step two and refine it into a working goal. Then you'll have an opportunity to work through steps one and two as many times as needed until you're ready to move to step three.

But for now, for step one, you need to let your hair down. More importantly, you need to put your guard down, because what I'm asking you to do—what you need to do before these other steps make sense—is figure out what you truly long for in life. Not just the whats, but the whys, too.

If you could do anything in the world—and know you would succeed—what would it be? Seriously. Dream big.

Okay, so the goal of step one is to get you to start dreaming and recording these outlandish dreams. Hopefully you're already good at this, but if you aren't, be sure to take the time to do this step right—no shortcuts here, no reality checks (just yet)—all we need are crazy dreams. And when I say crazy, I mean crazy!

WHY YOU'LL SETTLE

Some of you are already rolling your eyes and planning to skim through the rest of this chapter to get to the "practical stuff," as if you think you're above all this silly dreaming nonsense. Well, you're not.

Here's what's really going on: You're embarrassed. Or you're too proud, too practical, too scared, or too scarred to actually do the vulnerable, hopeful, yet unappreciated work of dreaming. You'll say that dreaming feels like a waste of time; what you mean is that you've had dreams crushed in the past and have trained yourself not to get your hopes up. Or maybe you feel that writing down your unfiltered dreams and owning them— declaring to the world that "this thing is my dream"—makes you feel delusional. Most of us would rather just skip the soul searching and get to the to-do list. But the truth is this: Living your dream starts with dreaming.

Steven Pressfield talks about that "craziness" that you are feeling. He calls it "resistance." (Remember the enemy within?) What you know you have to do brings about an equal, if not greater, internal struggle against it. It's this invisible "resistance" that has the ability to stop us in our tracks. We have a frustrating capacity to become our own worst critic and point out all the flaws in our plan, whether they are real flaws or not. In a sub-conscious effort to protect ourselves (a reflex often reinforced by past hurts and failures), we naturally resist putting ourselves out there.

Maybe all this dreaminess creeps you out and scares the

be-junk out of you. Maybe you're scared to acknowledge what's really inside your heart—scared people will think it's stupid or shoot it down. Scared you don't have what it takes to make it real. You think that if you can just bottle it up inside it'll be safe. No one goes crazy, no one's heart gets broken, and no one has a quarter- or midlife crisis and gives up on it all. Because, you reason, that is where unrealistic dreams and those who dream them end up: crushed by the reality of life. Dreaming is all well and good—until you wake up. Then it's a different story. In the end, you'd rather just dream safe, silly little dreams—or not dream at all—than risk a rude awakening by reality.

Honestly, there are few things scarier than truly facing your own dreams. Because once you acknowledge them, once you put them out there, you're accountable to them—and what you do from there on out feels like a pass-or-fail test with the whole world as your judge. So, rather than own our dreams and work as best we can toward them, we pretend like we don't have dreams at all so we don't feel bad when they don't come true. That resistance is natural, but you have to face those fears and take the risk of dreaming.

Because you always have "no"—but you might have "yes."

SHAKE IT UP

So here's the reality. If you don't shake it up, if you don't decide here and now to make a change, you'll never dare to dream audacious dreams, and you will probably never get to the root of what you really, truly want in life. Instead, you'll chase little half dreams around with mixed success and feel unsatisfied. So the choice is up to you. What will it be?

Go big or go home. Release all that fear and terror involved with defining something that most likely has been bouncing around your head for years. If you want to get the best out of yourself, you need to give yourself permission to think any-thing—no wrong answers. Don't prejudge or criticize yourself. And never, ever call yourself stupid. That's a lie. If you can't be open and honest with yourself, you're going to have a real hard time, not just in step one of my Patented Seven-Step Blueprint for Dream Job Fulfillment but well, in, all of life if we're being truthful.

This is your chance to dream. No judgment. No criticism. Just pure dreaming. And remember, this is for you—no one else even has to see this stuff. This is you, sitting at your desk in your job or in your living room at home. Relax. Just dream.

Here's the thing: I think you already know what your dream is. I think you know what you really, truly want to do. Hugh MacLeod calls this idea, this calling, your "private Mount Ever-est." I like the metaphor. And maybe it sounds crazy to talk about higher purposes and destinies and all that, but as you read this page, tell me you don't feel deep in your soul that you were meant to do something—something you've tried, with varying success, to ignore. It doesn't even have to be something particu-larly noble. In fact, you might feel like it's embarrassing or stu-pid, or like no one else would understand why it's important. But the important thing is that it's important to the only person who matters—you.

I want you to feel crazy about what you write down. Don't play it safe. At this point in the process, set aside what you think is reasonable or even possible. Put the bar out of reach. No one dreams of having "enough" money or being "moderately suc-cessful" or reaching "one" person. At the end of the day, maybe you would be content with those minimums—I don't know, but I'm betting not. But the truth is this: If it's safe and easy, it's not a dream. When we dream we paint a picture of what seems nearly impossible. If you aren't pushing the boundaries of what is sane, then you're not really dreaming. Period.

POSSIBLE HURDLES

Maybe this step is easy for you. Some of you have been recording and replaying your dreams for most of your life. Whatever it is that is still holding you back, it isn't a failure to clearly define your dream. You know exactly what you want and why you want it.

Others of you haven't got a clue. In fact, when I ask you, a few pages from now, to write something down, you may just write something you overheard someone say once on the phone in line at a Starbucks. You don't even know what it means; it just sounded vaguely important and professional. Really, all you know is that whatever you're doing right now isn't working out well and you want something different. You don't have a clear dream at all, which probably makes you feel bad about yourself, because what kind of pathetic person doesn't have a *dream* for crying out loud?

It's okay. You aren't a freak. In fact, like many people, you may discover you're just not a good dreamer. Most of us non-children aren't. Somewhere between kindergarten and college, most of us grow out of the innate ability we all enjoyed as kids to imagine elaborate and outrageous fantasies and to render never-before-seen colors across the canvas of our mind's eye. If you don't know what I'm talking about, visit just about any city park and you'll see what I mean. Just be careful not to act like a creeper.

Even if you already have a well-defined dream, are pretty sure you know what you want to pursue, and feel good about what you've written down, I'd encourage you to take the next questions and exercises seriously.

Oftentimes the past holds clues to what we desire in the present or have desired all along. (Remember our Jump GPS?) Take a minute to think back to your earliest dreams. Think back to your childhood dreams, when you wanted to be all kinds of improbable and impossible things: a superhero or an explorer or a princess or a spy or a kitty-cat or a knight or a Jedi. I had a friend who wanted to be a fire truck. Not a firefighter, a fire truck.

But beyond wanting to *be* incredible things, we also wanted to *do* incredible things. In our make-believe games, we could fly, were invisible, had healing powers, used force fields, and possessed every other magical ability we could dream up. Good always won. Nothing was impossible. Nothing. If we could imagine it, we could do it, and we could change whole worlds with a simple thought. For some of us, we dreamed of a day when things would be different for us—when we would be loved and listened to, when we would be safe, when we would have justice.

These early dreams are almost wishes. Often they don't really have much to do with any particular job, but they usually tell us a lot about what sorts of things have always appealed to us, the kind of environments or challenges we tend to gravitate toward, or even the sorts of causes that get us fired up. They were the things that captured our imagination.

While our own pasts often inspire our dreams, sometimes others inspire our dreams by what they've created and the stories they've told. An athlete, a song, a biography, a tragedy, a poem, a movie—inspiration is everywhere. Dreamers need to look to dreamers for inspiration.

Whether you've been inspired by your past or by some crazy idealist, it's important to recognize and understand the origin of your dream job—what it is that makes this particular situation or career so appealing to you. For some people, their dream is rooted in a fight for something they resonate with or a fight against something they've always felt is wrong. Some people's dream job was born out of feeling they had something to prove to others or even themselves. Others begin in a random moment of clarity, or in a flash of divine inspiration when they suddenly realize how well they're suited to a particular role or calling. Understanding the origin of your dream is the anchor that you must hold on to. Knowing why this goal, this dream, matters to you is your sanity—your anchor in the open sea after the jump.

Dream big, sure. But size doesn't really matter here. What matters is that the dream is *yours*.

MAKING THE JUMP

The world needs dreamers. Idealists. Visionaries. People unashamed to stand up and say audacious things like, "I want to end poverty in my lifetime." The world *needs* you.

The life of a dreamer is a difficult life. Sometimes it is a lonely life. And, without a doubt, a life marked by financial insecurity. (Maybe I should've mentioned this sooner . . .) But seriously, does anything worthwhile really come easy? If you think everything in life is going to come easy, you're lying to yourself. Period.

In 1910, Theodore Roosevelt delivered a speech at the Sorbonne in Paris:

> *It is not the critic who counts: not the man who points out how the strong man stumbles or where the doer of deeds could have done them better. The credit belongs to the man who is actually in the arena, whose face is marred by dust and sweat and blood; who strives valiantly; who errs and comes up short again and*

*again, because there is no effort without error or shortcoming;
but who knows the great enthusiasms, the great devotions; who
spends himself for a worthy cause; who, at the best, knows, in the
end, the triumph of high achievement, and who, at the worst, if
he fails, at least he fails while daring greatly, so that his place
shall never be with those cold and timid souls who knew neither
victory nor defeat.*

The world is full of critics. And you *will* be criticized for your
dreams. You need to learn, over time, how to be open to criticism
but also resilient to it, because you could receive enough criticism
to bury your dream forever. You need to be very, very careful
whom you receive your criticism from.

Your dream could be so many different things. You might
want to start a new nonprofit organization. You might want to
prototype a new product to sell. You might want to become an
actress or a model. You might want to become a professional
musician or an Olympic athlete. You might want to start a homeless shelter or provide clean water. You might want to work for
Apple, build bridges, design city parks, or run for Congress. You
might want to open your own store or start your own business.

I can tell you some wise words that TED Conferences founder
Richard Saul Wurman once said: "I don't have all the answers. I
just know some of the first things I would do."

So, here's your chance to shake it up and begin defining your
dream job. You're not going to type it—you're going to write it
on paper in your own handwriting. Because if you write it, you
own it—it's *your* dream. Use a pencil if you must, but remember,
there are no wrong answers here. Whether it fits on this paper or
you need to get your own piece of paper or a favorite moleskin, it
doesn't matter—just write it all down.

<u>My Dream</u>:

Great job! It may not have felt like a significant step now—
you may not even be all that proud of what you've written down
right now—but it's how this journey begins, and setting off in
the right direction makes all the difference in where you end up.

Now, if you actually managed to read to this point without
writing something down, you've missed the whole point. The
first key to seeing your dream come true is to tackle it as it's running through your head and drag it into the real world. So, in
answer to your excuse for not writing anything down: No, you
can't just "think about" your dream or "explain" your dream out
loud, because thoughts and sounds happen quickly in a moment
and then disappear and are forgotten. There is nothing more
definitive than writing your dream down. It exists in the physical world. If it helps you, pull out your smartphone and use it as
a voice recorder to get yourself started, but then I want you to
take that recording and *write your dream job down.*

Whatever your dream is, before you go any further, you need to go back and actually write something—*anything*—down. The rest of these steps are going to help you learn to clarify, expand, shape, dream bigger, etcetera, but we need to have something we can work from before we can move on.

All right, with that done, what are some things that can help you dream better and bigger? I'm glad you asked.

Be specific. Maybe you've heard the saying, "If you aim at nothing, you'll hit it every time." Well, it's true. Here's the thing: Vague ideas never happen. In fact, vagueness means certain failure. You can dream all you want, but if you aren't specific, you have nothing to aim for. Period. You can't just say that you want to "make a difference" or "be successful." It'll never happen. You need to put in the hard work to be specific. If there were a 100 percent chance that you'd succeed, what would you want to do? Seriously. The more specific you can be, the better and more likely it is to come true. Instead of letting your dream float around vaguely in the atmosphere, nail it down. Don't settle for a half-baked dream—if it's worth dreaming, it's worth putting in the effort. When you start to dream, start by answering the BIG questions—Who? What? When? Where? Why? How?

Make the complex clear. (Are you noticing a trend here?) Ask this question: What does this really look like? Don't settle for a quick little sentence about what you want to do and call it a day. Push yourself. Make sure that you leave nothing to the "wait and see" category, because the truth is this: If you take the approach of "wait and see," you might as well close the book and get back to living whatever kind of life you have now—your dream job will never happen. Don't take the shortcut. Keep pushing yourself. You need to be absolutely clear and leave nothing to ambiguity or chance. Again, the more clear and specific you can be in step one, the better—and the easier it will be when you move on to the other steps.

Make sure your dream is GPS-oriented. Remember, we're trying to use X and Y to help find Z. Take a few minutes to think over your past. Okay, now answer this: When was a time that you felt fully alive? How did it feel? What were you doing? Maybe you should listen to that memory, as it most likely has something to do with your dream. Face it. No one wants to cruise through life just getting by when they can do something extraordinary— something that makes them feel alive. You want to do something that energizes you, right? Something you love, right? Well, then find out where you've experienced those feelings in the past and follow that trail. If you're having a problem identifying anything, ask someone close to you what he or she thinks. Invite others to help you process what makes you fully alive.

What does success look like? It's not enough to merely state what you want to do and leave it at that. If you want your dream to really happen, you need to have some kind of an idea of what it looks like to succeed at it. Close your eyes and see it. What does success look like? What would it look like to be actually living your dream? See yourself actually *doing* it, actually living your dream. What do you see? Again, if you have no idea what it looks like, it's not going to happen. Take the time here in step one to really get a hold of what it is that you want to do. If you have any doubt, keep working, keep dreaming, and keep pressing forward until you arrive at something that really gets you going.

Take money out of the equation. All right, this may sound kind of crazy, but here goes. If your bank account were full of money, what would motivate you to still get up every day and go to work? In other words, what would you do for work, even if you weren't getting paid for it? Now don't get me wrong, I'm not saying that you should totally forget about the financial side and just jump blindly—you need to eat. What I am saying is that you need to check your heart and see what makes you come alive— something that you'd do for the love of it. When you absolutely love what you do, your dream job becomes, well, a dream come true.

Make your dream visual. If you want to be successful, you can't just write down your dream and stuff it in a drawer with used batteries, paper clips, or whatever else you keep in there. You need to keep your dream in front of you visually. Maybe you want to create a fictional article or a press release announcing your achievement. Maybe you want to find some photos of someone who is living your dream and post them somewhere prominent. Perhaps you might want to start collecting articles about your dream job—like interviews with people who have succeeded at attaining your dream job. Whatever it is, make it visual. Have something that you can look at every day that will inspire you to keep pressing forward. Trust me— you're going to need it!

TALES OF THE JUMP

Ben Arment knows a lot about dreams. A few years ago, he founded STORY, an innovative two-day conference held in downtown Chicago that focuses on providing inspiration for the creative class. Besides founding STORY, Ben also founded Dream Year, an annual program that takes twelve individuals through the process of realizing their dreams. Essentially, Ben has devoted his life to assisting people in carrying out their true purpose in life, which is why he was a perfect person to talk to about realizing the first step.

What did you used to do?

I used to work for other people. An advertising copywriter. A newspaper reporter. A minister. And, finally, an event producer.

I thought I was doing things I loved. But when frustration keeps creeping into every role, there's something amiss at the very root of it all. It took me a while to figure this out.

What did you want to do?
I wanted to work for myself. I wanted to create experiences for people—whether they're films, concerts, events, or conferences. But I wanted them to be expressions of my creative ideas, not just services for other people. And I wanted them to change. Projects to start and stop. I wanted to produce numerous ideas, not just one.

What was it that made you realize it was time for a change?
Office politics did me in. I hated trying to look busy on Friday afternoons at 3:00 P.M. when no one was actually working. I was tired of trying to please a boss who could not be pleased. I felt like the crew member on a sailing ship whose course was changed each week by the whims of my boss. And I was tired of having great ideas vetoed by the lack of imagination in other people. I wanted my own laboratory in which to fail or succeed.

What initially kept you from pursuing your dream job? What resistance (internal or external) did you face?
I had been trained my whole life to be an employee. That's what you're taught in school—to work for other people, to clock in and clock out, to do your duty, to not make a ruckus, to not fail. So I was afraid to go out on my own. When I first learned I had permission to start something, it opened my eyes to a whole new world. When I learned that I could make money from starting something, I could do nothing else.

When you were a child, what did you dream of becoming when you grew up? How did your dreams change over time?
I dreamed of running an ice cream parlor. It was going to be called the Cocoa Nut Hut and serve thousands of people on hot summer nights. It was going to be situated in the woods with a large deck surrounded by trees. But as I grew up, my world got larger, and I no longer wanted to be confined to a small-town shop. I wanted to dabble in more epic ideas. It turns out that coming up with the idea of the Cocoa Nut Hut was actually more exciting than running the shop myself.

How did you know when you'd found your dream job?
I knew that I'd found my dream job when I was executing my own ideas and earning a salary larger than what other jobs had paid me. I'm all for sacrificing to do what you love. But that's completely unnecessary if you can find the place where your passions match up with market demand.

Why did you want to work in the field you're in?
I wanted to create experiences because I am moved so deeply by them myself. Everywhere I go, I pay attention to sensory experiences, from the music in the background and the manufactured smells to the texture of paper and the tone of voices. You can integrate all of these elements to produce a particular emotion or response. I wanted to orchestrate this total experience.

What experiences in your past most significantly shaped your career choices?
I was born to produce events. From a very early age, I was producing shows for my family in the living room. My children's minister was a Barnum and Bailey–trained circus clown, which

inspired me to dream bigger. In my teens, I got to help a production team with a national concert tour when it rolled through town. This made big events seem possible to me—even very doable. When I started producing events on my own, I had some early successes, which kept me in the game until I could gain real experience and learn how to make it profitable.

What influence have your hobbies, skills, beliefs, or personality traits had on your career choices?

Whenever people describe a project, a mental to-do list immediately forms in my head. I can't help it. It just happens. This is the part of my personality I don't understand but am thankful to have. Producing comes easily to me because I can see the individual parts that make up a whole and I can anticipate where things might go wrong. I suppose the answer lies somewhere between Myers-Briggs, StrengthsFinder, and all of those other personality assessments.

What is your muse? What keeps you moving forward?

I am carried forward by the power of ideas. Right now, I'm conspiring with several friends to produce a movie-themed event in our home city. It's the combination of a movie premiere, a costume party, and a theatrical show. I wrote a screenplay several months ago that I'd love to turn into a film. And I've booked the House of Blues in Chicago next fall for an event that's to be determined. Ideas are my consuming passion.

Step Two: Refine Your Dream Job

"Would you tell me, please, which way I ought to walk
from here?"
"That depends a good deal on where you want to get to,"
said the Cat.
"I don't much care where—" said Alice.
"Then it doesn't matter which way you walk," said the
Cat.
"—so long as I get somewhere," Alice added as an explana-
tion.
"Oh, you're sure to do that, "said the Cat, "if you only walk
long enough."

—LEWIS CARROLL, *Alice in Wonderland*

If you've moved on to step two without writing something down, this next bit—indeed, the rest of this book—is going to be useless to you. Let me put it this way: If you don't have the guts or discipline to write your dream job down, there's no way you're going to have the guts or discipline to actually make it happen. Flip back a few pages and write something down or close the book and get on with your life. Otherwise, you're just playing games with yourself and wasting your own time.

Once you've allowed yourself to dream without fear of criticism—once you've fully opened yourself to the world of possibilities and examined what you deeply, truly long for in life, it's time to move on to step two.

Step two isn't free-form and fanciful like step one, but it tends to come more naturally to most of us. This is where you reexamine and refine your dream through the lens of reality. If step one is the heart of your dream—what ignites your passions and stirs your deepest longings, hopes, and desires—then step two is the brain. Step two brings focus, clarity, and shape to your dream—or else discards it altogether. Only the best dreams survive step two.

At this point, your dream job is probably too broadly defined or too vague to be of any real use to you. Or maybe it's too complex or too far removed to serve as any kind of tangible goal. If you want to get there eventually, you'll need to start smaller, simpler, and smarter.

The dream job you defined in step one should drive and guide everything else, but it isn't nearly enough on its own to take you to the end. Wishful thinking is not a strategy. Hopes and desires can't substitute for details and plans.

It's time to get practical.

DO THIS STEP OR ELSE

As much as many of us would love to live in the exuberant glow of step one forever, sooner or later (sooner is usually better), it's time to face certain facts: some dreams are, sadly, out of reach. I wish I could tell you that nothing is impossible, but there is a heap of evidence to the contrary. Remember my childhood friend who wanted to be a fire truck? Sorry, kid, that's just not in the cards. It's not going to happen.

Step two is critical because this is where you ask yourself the hard questions. Questions like: "What is this job really like?" "What skills are required, and do I have them?" "If not, can I learn?" "Can I really make a living doing this?" "What will it cost to pursue this?" "Am I really willing to do what it takes to make this dream happen?" "What do you mean, 'Santa isn't real'?" Failure to ask—and answer—these questions now could trip you up big-time down the road. There are few things sadder than seeing someone invest tons of time and energy into a dream that, at the end of the day, doesn't really have a chance to survive.

Step two is all about carefully considering each dream in the light of day, about narrowing down and refining the endless possibilities that excite you into a dream you can actually pursue.

This is where you begin to figure out exactly how far you must go and what it will cost to get there. Not until after you've done the hard research will you know if your dream job is actually a viable goal—or if it's even worth it to you.

So, I have a challenge for you:

Talk Yourself Out of Your Dream Job

Maybe you can't. That's great—you might have caught a keeper. But I want you to try nonetheless—and I want you to give it everything you've got. Why? Because if you can talk yourself out of your dream job, you probably don't want it badly enough. If you have (or uncover) good reasons not to pursue this, it's best to face them and face them soon. Write it off and start over. There's nothing heroic about forcing it. That's pretty much the opposite of what we're all about here.

The truth of the matter is this: You must confront reality now. Otherwise, you run the risk of falling in love with and chasing after the fantasy version of your dream job and not the real thing. You'll end up as the guy with a "great" job who actually hates what he does. What sounds good in theory often looks like crap when it comes right down to it.

Before you invest time, money, sweat, and tears into making this thing happen, you have to know it's achievable. You have to know, beyond a shadow of a doubt, that it's really, truly what you want to pursue.

A lot of people get hung up here because they start overthinking it. Sure, step two is about figuring out if you really, truly want this specific dream job, but it's important to keep in mind that we're not talking about forever here. Don't measure your specific dream job against what you want in a "for the rest of your life" sort of way—dreams often evolve over time and that's to be expected. You're not sealing your fate or locking yourself into anything. What you are doing is this: You are starting down a path that is going to take some serious time and commitment, so you better be darn sure you want to arrive at the destination and stay there for a while.

It's simple enough: If you don't like the band, don't go to the concert. And if you don't know whether or not you like the band, listen to their music. Ignorance is an excuse that step two eliminates. Do your research and decide. Is this truly what you want to pursue or not?

WHY YOU'LL SETTLE

For some of you, step two is going to be easy for all the wrong reasons. You've been talking yourself out of pursuing your dreams for good "practical" reasons your entire life. The voice inside your head, the one that tells you "it can't be done," is loud and persistent and kicks butt at cross-examinations.

It's also a liar.

Seriously. It's the devil. Call it resistance, call it ghosts, call it anything but helpful counsel. What you're hearing, my friends, is the sound of settling.

For others of you, the enemy within will sing a much different tune at step two, because it's a cunning little saboteur. Some of you won't hear criticism at all. You won't be able to think of a single reason not to pursue your dream. It's perfect. You feel good about it. There's no resistance whatsoever. Let's do this!

Be afraid. Be very afraid.

If something inside you doesn't raise concerns or seek desperately for a good excuse to wimp out, you're probably not onto something amazing—you're probably way far off base. Here's the thing: If it's a good dream, you will face resistance. You will want to settle. The only times you don't feel the pull to settle are when you're already settling. The only times you don't feel resistance are when you're doing something selfish or boring or self-destructive. Those things come easy. In my previous book, I talked about how villains don't attack people who aren't threats. If you're not getting pushback, you're either blind, bad, or beaten—or maybe all of them.

If it feels like a brilliant idea, it probably isn't. If it sounds like an easy win, it probably isn't. Don't be fooled. Don't do it for the glory. Look for dreams that have resistance, because when you do, you're onto something.

Either way, in step two, you'll settle because you're afraid to face the facts. We choose not to face the facts because we're afraid of the truth. Oftentimes it's just easier to quit dreaming than to examine the dream closely. You suspect the challenge will prove too hard, so you don't bother investigating. Or you falsely believe it will be easier than it is and would prefer getting started right away rather than doing your homework.

Get on the scale. Balance your checkbook. Ask the hard

questions and don't wallow in self-pity and despair when you find the answers.

SHAKE IT UP

Before we get too much further, I need to say something you're not going to want to hear: Sometimes you can't just follow your passion.

Much has been written (in recent years, at least) about turning your passion into a full-time job. I mean, that's the dream, right? Get paid for doing what you love.

Well, the situation is actually a little more complicated than that. Can you make a living doing what you love? Yes . . . and no. To be honest with you, it depends. Not every passion or every dream or everything you love to do has profit potential. Some dreams and some hobbies make lousy businesses. Professional careers don't exist for some of this stuff and it'd be tough going getting something started.

The trick is finding that sweet spot where what you love to do and what other people want overlap. Opportunity lies at the point where your passion and its usefulness to other people converge.

See, for a business to exist there have to be at least two things: a product or service and people willing to pay for it. If what you love to do isn't useful to anyone else—if it doesn't create value for other people by solving an obvious and irritating problem or bestowing some desirable benefit—then you're probably never going to make money doing it. Passion isn't enough if there's no business potential.

That said, it's almost always possible to find a career (or make your own) in an area closely related to something you love.

No one is going to pay you to read books for fun, but there are plenty of jobs—book editor, patent lawyer, proposal writer, reviewer/critic, researcher—that require a great deal of reading.

No one is going to pay you for working in your garden or taking care of your own lawn, but they might be interested in buying your flowers or produce or in learning how to create and tend their own garden. There's the opportunity.

The question then becomes: Are any of the opportunities related to what you love interesting to you? If so, dig deeper. If not, pick something else you enjoy and explore the possibilities there.

If you're thinking about starting your own business based on a hobby or personal passion, answering these questions before you continue will help you figure out if the business is really something you'd enjoy and if there's really a market for it.

- Would you enjoy pursuing your hobby/passion full-time, or at least twenty hours a week?
- Do you enjoy teaching others to practice the same hobby/share the same passion?
- Do you like all the details of your hobby, even the parts other people find tedious or boring or difficult?
- If your hobby/passion required a decent amount of administrative work, would you still enjoy it?
- If your paycheck depended on pursuing your hobby/passion, would you still enjoy it?
- Have other people asked for your help related to your hobby/passion?
- Are there enough people out there willing to pay to benefit from your expertise?
- Are there other businesses serving this market? Would you be able to serve this market better?

It's All About the Research

Whether you dream of bringing a new product to market or getting hired at Google, you need to become an expert on everything related to your dream job. You'll look like a fool in step three if you don't do this work now.

Say in step one you wrote down that you want to own a coffee shop. Okay. Now, what does that look like? What does it actually mean—what does it actually *require* to own your own coffee shop? Do you know anything about beans, farming, and growing regions? Do you know anything about different roasting, grinding, and brewing methods? Do you know anything about running a retail business? Do you know if there's a market for a coffee shop in your area? Do you know what you could expect to earn running a coffee shop? Do you know anything about management? hiring? customer service? Do you know anything about FDA certification? If not, it's time to learn.

As you think about your dream job and begin to refine it, here's what you need to know:

- The history of the company, business, or product
- The education requirements and potential cost
- The working environment or physical location
- The tools of the trade
- The typical pay you can expect when starting out
- The typical benefits you can expect when starting out
- The time requirements needed to be successful
- The physical requirements
- The skills requirements needed
- The emotional, relational, and physical costs
- The laws and legal issues associated with the job

Intimidated? Allow me to introduce your new best friend— the Internet. Google is your best friend in step two. So much information is available to you today, and much of it is free and can be accessed within three minutes. And don't forget to take advantage of your local library as well. There's much to be learned from books.

In the end, these questions should challenge you, not defeat you. If these questions challenge your dream and it remains standing—it's worth pursuing. If these questions defeat you, you need to ask yourself why. Are you settling? Are you giving up? Or have you simply discovered you've been barking up the wrong tree?

There's no shame in turning back to step one if you're on the wrong trail.

Do You Have What It Takes?

Once you've thoroughly investigated the ins and outs of your particular dream job, it's time to turn your questions inward. Now that you know what your dream job requires, you must face the reality of whether or not you have what it takes to do it.

Maybe you've realized in your research that your dream job requires you to perform tasks that you take no pleasure in whatsoever, or that it requires you to work in an environment you simply don't like.

Sometimes poor health, injury, or disability will make it next to impossible to successfully pursue your dream. Sometimes you'll simply lack the natural ability your dream job requires, and no amount of education or training will be able to compensate.

This is a great place to flip back to the section on "Finding Yourself (Part Two)" for a second and reexamine your identity. How well do your interests, skills, beliefs, and unique qualities line up with the nuts and bolts of your chosen dream?

This is really hard to do objectively, because we like to think we can do anything we set our minds to. We can't. Sometimes we're being delusional, and it's obvious to everyone else but us. To everyone else, it's sad and strangely fascinating (like virtually every show on TLC) to watch a person cling feverishly to an impossible dream out of unwillingness to accept that it isn't for them. It's like watching the first few weeks of a new season of *American Idol,* where all the desperate, starry-eyed dreamers without any natural ability parade themselves before the public eye declaring themselves to be the next American idol. Then, one by one, they open their mouths and the truth comes out— it's instantly apparent this person is not a good match for their dream. No one will ever pay them to sing; anyone with working ears could make that call accurately.

Now, they might genuinely enjoy singing; after all, you don't have to be good at something to take some pleasure in it, and no one but you can ultimately judge what you do or do not like to do. But something you're bad or even just average at will probably never form the core of your dream job.

What's most astonishing to me in these open-audition scenarios is how many people refuse to accept reality. The judges literally cringe when they hear the contestant caterwaul into a microphone, ask them to please stop, and kindly dismiss them from the competition. At this point, belligerently insisting that, no, you are in fact very, very talented despite whatever people may say, doesn't make you look resolved. Doesn't make people think, *Ah, there's a fighter!* No. It makes you look pathetic.

Don't be pathetic. If you've latched onto a dream that is clearly unsuitable, face the facts and let it go. If it's a bad fit, guess what? It was never meant to be your dream. You'll never be called to something you're completely incapable of doing well. You may want something you're not cut out for, but that doesn't mean it's a good dream, or one that would even make you ultimately happy and satisfied with life.

This brings us to the step two question that trumps them all.

Why Do You Want This?

Take the first answer that pops into your head and write it down. Examine it. Ask yourself if it's true. Why is achieving this so important to you?

When most people get to step two, the kinds of questions they ask are shallow and irrelevant: "How much money will I make?" "Will I look cool?" "Will it impress so and so?" "Will it make my dad proud?"

Stop. Start over. Those are stupid reasons to jump. You're chasing a stupid dream. Don't do it for status. Don't marry yourself to an idea for the wrong reasons—because it's cool or sexy or sounds important or gives you an excuse for tooling around and telling crazy stories and griping about how hard it is and how tortured you are. If you don't have anything to say, shut up. If you don't have a vision, or don't have talent, don't fake it. Don't be a poser because you're jealous, because you feel that somehow your lot in life—your particular interests, passion, calling, or dream—isn't good enough. You've got to stay true to your heart. Be you. You'll be good at that if you try.

You have to dig deep and face your own motives and set your own priorities. What are you really trying to accomplish here?

Again: Would you do this if there was no payoff?

You might be better off starting this journey on the assumption that you will not be rewarded for your efforts. Seriously. Imagine zero payoff. Imagine you land your dream job, and, as a result, you work longer hours, get paid less than you do now, and lose the respect of all your peers. Is it still appealing to you? Do you still want it?

If the answer is yes, go on.

Sometimes it's helpful at this point to invite feedback from other people. Somehow just talking about your dream out loud makes it feel more real. It's "out there." Other people know. They can help you think through options you may have missed or point out strengths or struggles or other factors that might indicate whether or not the dream you're beginning to refine is taking a shape suitable for you.

But remember, nobody cares about your dream the same way you do. Do it for yourself. If you're jumping after this dream for somebody else, you will fail. And you'll be miserable in the meantime.

So don't lean *too* heavily on others' advice about or reactions to your dream, especially at first. The best way to get approval is to not need it. Nobody can tell you if what you're doing is good, meaningful, or worthwhile. You don't need anyone's approval, and the road will be lonely at times. Dreams tend to challenge the status quo and shake things up. Anyone close to you will be affected by your dream, and, remember, settling is natural. It's easier if things stay the same. At the heart of a dream is change, and few people *really* get excited about that. More often than not, people feel threatened when you question the way things are and suggest it could be better. It's that weak, craven, lazy-butt part of a person that resists your dreams at first and urges you to be careful.

When it comes to dreams and self-expression, there is rarely such a thing as "too risky." Some friends of mine were talking about this portfolio review they attended. A couple of local design professionals had gathered to offer feedback to whoever wanted it, and a bunch of artists and designers at various stages of education with varied levels of talent showed up to take them up on the offer. One young woman who freelanced as a graphic designer scrolled through her portfolio, describing some of the cards and logos and other graphics she'd put together. Frankly, they were boring—not without skill, but nothing my friend hadn't already seen a billion unmemorable times in the templates and clip-art galleries of preinstalled software. But here's the thing that was memorable: She stopped halfway through and said, "Sometimes I feel like my designs are too out there." She was so afraid of making something uncommercial, something people wouldn't like, that she made something uninteresting and, as it happens, something people *didn't* like. She sold out with nothing to sell.

Don't tone it down. Stay true to yourself. Don't worry about other people or concern yourself with who is or who isn't a sell-out. Don't distract yourself with observations about overlooked geniuses and overfamous imbeciles. Their path, their success or failure, deserved or not, has no actual bearing on the real question: What are *you* going to do with the short time you have left on the earth? With or without the help or attention of the world at large, what are you going to do?

POSSIBLE HURDLES

Our dreams are typically more ambitious than we realize. They always seem to require a higher level of quality, higher level of commitment, higher level of training, longer hours, bigger sacrifices than we consider at first.

This is why step two is so critical. If you really want a shot at living your dream, you have to do your homework. You have to know the requirements and the cost of your dream. I said it before: If you fail to ask—and answer—the hard questions, you're going to find yourself inadequately equipped to chase your dream. Like finding yourself on a long journey without a map.

But something else can happen if you don't count the cost of your dream—you'll quit. You'll give up because it's just too hard, or just too much, or just too whatever. You'll find every excuse, every reason why you can't make it, why you can't live your dream. You'll wake up one day, right in the middle of chasing your dream, and cash it in because you didn't do your homework and jump with eyes wide open about what it was going to take. You came up with a dream but didn't prepare for the long haul—and now you've quit.

Don't let that happen to you—your dream, your life are way too important to leave to chance and half-baked planning. Do your homework. Ask the hard questions. Learn as much as you can about what it is going to take to make your dream happen. If you want to be a designer, learn everything you can about being a designer. If you want to open a coffee shop or be a writer, a graphic artist, a litigator, whatever it may be—learn everything you can about the requirements, the costs, the education and experience needed to see your dream really happen. What you will find is a blueprint for helping you make your dream happen. Without step two, your dream has a possibility but not a probability of happening. Don't get me wrong, it's still a good dream, but it's just not one that is worth jumping for—yet.

The last step in this journey is mastering and mentoring. I'll tell you right now, it takes a long time to become a master. All you need to worry about now is starting off on the right foot.

MAKING THE JUMP

You've done your research. You've brought your dream out of the ether and wrapped it in reality. What remains is tangible. Something worth jumping for.

You'll continue to refine your dream over time, but you're circling in on it now. You're pinpointing the target, specifying the exact destination of this journey. It's time to write a refined version of your dream. Here's your chance. Knowing what you know now—having asked yourself all the questions posed by this chapter, what does your dream look like? You have a lot of new information at your disposal, so be as specific as you can be.

My Dream (In Detail):

Steps one and two can be repeated as many times as necessary to land a dream job that feels like a good fit and stands up under investigation. Don't move forward until you're ready.

Embrace your limitations, focus on your strengths, sing in your own voice, ignore the critics, stop making excuses, and get ready to keep working your tail off.

That's it. There she is. Go get her, tiger.

TALES OF THE JUMP

Ryan Duffy was a pilot in the navy for nine and a half years before he made a transition to the "real" world. He had attended the prestigious U. S. Naval Academy and knew upon graduation that he would be obligated to serve in the armed forces, but he wasn't always sure that he could be a career navy man. Three years into the service, at the age of twenty-six, he had decided that he didn't want to fly for the rest of his working life.

At that point, Ryan began to seek other career possibilities. Through that process, he landed on the law.

Tell us a bit about your transition.

The navy was a great experience, but I wasn't passionate about flying. Some people find this hard to believe, but that was the truth for me. I wanted something that would challenge me in a more academic fashion, yet where I could still be forced to think on my feet. Additionally, I wouldn't have to deploy away from my family. I did face some resistance to this "plan" of mine. Most people could not understand why I didn't love to fly and thought I was crazy to be walking away from a large signing bonus and a very safe and secure paycheck.

After you decided what your dream job actually was, what sort of research did you do to determine if the job was a fit for you?

Most of the research I did was hands-on. I found any lawyer I could to talk to. I would pick their brain as to what their work was like and how they did their job. I especially wanted to know what their day-to-day life was like. If this was the job I was headed for, I needed all the information I could get.

Usually, I ended each interview session by asking for names of other lawyers who might be willing to give me advice. My goal was to get at least one additional name for every person I talked to. You'd be surprised how many people are willing to help, especially when it's just a few minutes to talk through their career choices.

What sort of feedback did you get from the people around you? Did anyone try and talk you out of it? Did you try and talk yourself out of it?
I have to say that I did receive more negative feedback than positive. A majority of the lawyers I spoke with tried to talk me out of it. The economy is too tough, the hours are long, or most lawyers aren't that happy with the time they put in. These were the comments I would get when speaking with other lawyers. Don't get me wrong, there were people who had great things to say about the job.

Other people outside the law tried to discourage me. As I said before, people could not understand why I would risk walking away from a secure job (not only secure, but sexy in a Tom Cruise sort of way) just to go back to school and start all over. When you hear people talk like this over and over, you can't help but doubt your decision. Yet when you know, you just know. After an enormous amount of research and time in prayer, I knew it was a risk worth taking. I heard somewhere that a person spends more time working than anything else. If that is true, then I figured I'd better be doing something I love.

How did the research process narrow your focus?
After speaking with many people and reading anything I could get my hands on, I decided I should start focusing on making a

plan and then executing it. Particularly, I needed to decide which law school to attend and what type of law I wanted to practice. There were dozens of factors, everything from finances to taking steps to network in the right area of law. Being a bit of a type A personality, I made a detailed plan and saw it through.

I really can't tell you how much the research helped, though. Listening to the thoughts of others can't replace personal experience, but the more you can internalize advice, the better off you'll be. It helps mitigate the frustration of obstacles when you can recognize a situation and say, "Oh, this is what interview subject number fourteen went through, and this is how they overcame this obstacle." Learning the experience of others won't necessarily make things easier, but it'll prepare you for when things get rough and your plan needs improvisation.

Currently, Ryan is practicing law and enjoying his new career immensely. That's not to say it's always easy. There are times the pressures of Ryan's new life wear on him, and there are times he is forced to remind himself that being a lawyer was the goal he wanted to pursue. It's important to remember that making the jump doesn't resolve everything, that reaching new life goals is a process that never really ends.

Step Three: Test-Drive Your Dream Job

All right! It seems you're onto something. You've done your due diligence in steps one and two, and, on paper at least, you have a dream that's yours, that seems to fit your calling and your skills. You believe (with good reason) that it's within your power to achieve it, and you've counted the cost and decided it's worth it. This is huge.

But before you can move onto steps four, five, six, and seven, there's one more thing to do: Put your dream to the test.

Steps one and two mostly take place in your head or on paper. Step three happens in the real world. Step three is where you start to get your hands dirty.

Sometimes there are things about a career you can't know until you actually jump in and get your feet wet. Fortunately, you can try just about anything before you jump, and testing the waters is a very, very smart idea, even if you're convinced a particular career is for you.

DO THIS STEP OR ELSE

Most people skip this step. A lot of those people are now reading this book, looking for a way out of the mess they've walked into. Perhaps you're one of them.

Step three is about confirming—or denying—what you've discovered in steps one and two. Depending on how it goes, it could send you back to square one. That might sound discouraging, but it's actually a whole lot better than getting all the way into step six before you realize you made a mistake—again.

Theory Versus Practice

For a brief moment in high school, I was convinced I wanted to be a doctor. I don't remember where that dream came from, but I do remember doing some initial research, step-two style. I knew that becoming a doctor would mean a lengthy stay in the halls of higher education, and I knew I'd have to study really hard for a long time, even in certain subjects where I showed no particular aptitude. But I'd convinced myself I could do it. I'd become generally interested in health and knew I liked working with people, so that seemed like a good fit. In the end, for me, the payoff sounded worth it: the title, the prestige, the projected annual earnings, and the cool white coat—not to mention the good feelings that come from helping people for a living. I was sold.

But before packing me off to school to pursue a premed major with their blessing and a pat on the head, my foster parents encouraged me to take an extra step and test the waters a bit further. They helped me arrange to spend a day in a doctor's office, following an actual doctor around and seeing firsthand what a career as a doctor really looked like.

It was one of the best days of my life, because it taught me how badly I *didn't* want to be a doctor. The smells, the sick people, the endless forms and files and charts and claims and antiseptic wipes—I hated it. I hadn't been there more than twenty minutes before I knew this whole doctor thing wasn't for me.

Did all the doctor career plans I'd been making up to that

point feel like a waste after that? Not really. I felt like I'd dodged a bullet. If I hadn't gone all step three on this doctor dream of mine, I could've slogged through several years of higher education, retaking anatomy and physiology over and over again before ever realizing the career that had sounded so perfect in theory was actually a bad fit for me in practice. Whew. I was relieved.

The same principle we learned in step two applies here as well: The sooner you can figure out that a particular dream job isn't actually a good fit, the less time you'll waste chasing it and the sooner you'll be able to find and invest in a dream that's actually worth it.

WHY YOU'LL SETTLE

You'll get stuck here for a billion stupid reasons, most of them sounding like some variation on your being too busy, or other people's being too busy, or your not finding the right opportunity. You'll wait around forever for that perfect connection or lucky break to open some magic door for you to walk through.

All the while you haven't opened your mouth or lifted a finger to actually make something happen.

What's really going on is that step three is making this whole jumping-ship thing kind of real, and you're freaking out a little. Right now, everything looks so pretty and perfect on paper that you're afraid to spoil it all by putting it to the test. More specifically, you're afraid of putting *yourself* to the test. You're afraid of change. You're afraid you'll love it and get your hopes up. You're afraid you'll hate it and feel like a failure for even dreaming it. You're even afraid of success, because then you have no excuses to hide behind—one less unknown standing between you and the future you think you want but are afraid to claim.

You're afraid of looking foolish. Perhaps you're too proud to ask for help or to "start over" at the bottom of this new ladder you hope to climb.

The reality is, you have absolutely nothing to lose in step three and tons and tons of really valuable things to learn, whether you end up more excited about your dream or find yourself walking back to the drawing board and starting over. Bottom line: When you've taken your dream for a test run, you'll know for sure, one way or the other, whether you're on the right track. If it turns out you're on the right track, it's super inspiring—you now know, really know, what you'll be working toward. If it turns out you've been on the wrong track, that's actually encouraging, too. Now you know that that dream isn't worth pursuing, that it doesn't make you come alive like you thought it would. Eliminating another wrong thing puts you that much closer to figuring out that right thing.

You've got to be ready to take advantage of the opportunities that will arise when you start getting your hands dirty. If you didn't spend enough time in step two doing your research, step three will expose you as a hack. If you did step two well, you should have little to fear in step three. You know what you're in for.

SHAKE IT UP

There are a few ways to test-drive your dream job and almost every one of them starts with other people. Up until now you could have kept your dreams pretty much between you, your notebook, your Google search history, and a few trusted friends. Not anymore. It's time to reach out. It's time to actually open your mouth and take a physical step toward living your future. Here are some steps you could take:

> *Interviewing:* Find some people who are living your dream
> right now and learn all you can from them.

Shadowing: Look out for opportunities to follow someone for a day—someone who is actually living your dream. (Think about my experience in the doctor's office and you'll get what I mean.)

Volunteering: Offer your time, free of charge, doing something, anything, that gets you close to those living your dream.

Internships: Investigate if there is a formal or informal internship you can apply for.

Mentorship/Apprenticeship: Perhaps one of the people you interview would be interested in pouring some time and expertise into you. Remember the saying from earlier: You always have "no"—but you might have "yes."

Practical Experience: Again, anything you can do that offers you practical, hands-on, real-life experience in your desired field of work is a win when it comes to making your dream job happen.

I'll talk about each of these a little, but I always recommend that people start step three the same way: by making a list of people who have your dream job. They don't have to be people you already know; in just a few minutes on the Internet— reaching out to friends, scouring Facebook and Twitter, or even doing a Google search—you can develop a list of a dozen people who are living your dream job. These are the people with the knowledge and experience you need to succeed. The question is whether or not you will seek them out and tap into what they know.

Once you have your list of people, break out the old research skills you polished in step two and get to work learning everything you can about them. Study their success. If they have a blog, read it. If they've written books or articles, read them. If books or articles have been written about them, read those, too. If they've been interviewed online, on air, or on TV, watch the video clips or read the transcripts. Follow them on Twitter. Like them on Facebook. Stalk them in the streets if you have opportunity. In all of this, pay special attention to their origin story; you may have chosen these people because you admire their current work, but you're studying them to learn as much as you can about *how they got there.*

Getting your dream job is always a process—a journey. Find out what theirs was and learn everything you can from their experience. Look for similarities between your personalities, interests, education, skills, etcetera and notice where you're different.

Finally, and most importantly, find their contact information. Once you've gathered all the public information that's available online or in print, it's time to introduce yourself.

Unless the person you've been stalking/admiring from afar has clearly indicated a different preference, I always recommend sending them a piece of snail mail. Snail mail tends to stand out from the crowd these days and cuts through the clutter of e-mail. It's also simultaneously more personal and more formal than other forms of communication and indicates a great deal more thoughtfulness than an e-mail. Sending snail mail takes some effort and requires some expense to send. That doesn't go unnoticed. Before they even open the envelope, you've indicated that you're serious.

A couple of important notes:

- Keep it short: Don't waste their time. Get right to the point.
- Don't go all fan-crazy on them, and don't talk about how great you are, either. Stay humble without groveling.

All you need to do is introduce yourself and ask for an informal ten-minute chat. You could try writing something like this:

> Dear [Their Name],
>
> My name is [Your Name]. You don't know me, but I admire your work as a [their work] and have been thinking about moving down a similar path. I know I have much to learn. I also know you are busy, but if you can spare even just ten minutes I would love to chat with you briefly and hear what you've learned along your journey. Thank you!
>
> Sincerely,
> [Your Name]
> [your phone number]

Easy enough, right? Your goal here is to meet with three professionals who have your dream job and ask them the questions you asked yourself in step two. Don't waste their time asking questions you've already found the answers to online. And be sure to ask them directly: "What advice would you give to yourself today if you were just starting out?"

Of course, you may not get to the stage where you're actually having conversations with these people for a while. It's highly possible you'll send off your little note and never hear anything back. Or their assistant will send you a nice "thanks for your note but please don't bother us anymore" card. That's okay. For one, you need to get used to facing potential rejection. For another, you've just learned a lesson about mastering and mentoring in your dream job—one that you should tuck away and refer to again when you get to step seven.

It is through these initial three conversations that you'll

pursue additional opportunities to test-drive your dream job. Ask your new contacts about volunteer or internship opportunities with them or someone else they'd recommend. Maybe they're willing to take you on as an apprentice or would consider mentoring you. Finding a mentor in step three is not absolutely essential, but it's a huge, huge plus, and you'll come out ahead in the end if you do.

POSSIBLE HURDLES

Your biggest hurdle in step three is lack of preparation. If you had the chance to try on your dream right now, would you blow it? Do you want things you aren't prepared for?

The hard truth is that you're not entitled to your dream job. You don't just get to have it because you want it. The universe doesn't owe you anything and won't simply hand you the job you want because it is obviously perfect for you and would make you happy.

We have this weird idea that people somehow "luck" into their dream jobs. We've all heard stories of people who just got lucky. They had a half-formed dream and barely made plans and *poof!* Acting career. Or we've heard of people who have dream jobs sort of thrust upon them out of nowhere, without even needing to look for them. Like supermodel Gisele Bündchen— allegedly, she was noticed by an elite modeling agent at a McDonalds and asked if she wanted to be a model. She said yes and went on to become the highest paid Victoria's Secret model in history and marry Patriots star quarterback Tom Brady. Not bad.

We like these stories because we're lazy, lotto-minded people who naturally prefer to win something rather than to struggle for it. We like to believe achieving our dreams is as easy as waiting for a stroke of luck to break into our lives and change our fortunes. We also like to pretend that "bad luck" is what's keeping us from living our dreams. We would've been successful a long time ago, we're certain, if only our luck would change. "I'm still waiting for my lucky break!" we tell ourselves. "Better luck next time." "I just wasn't in the right place at the right time, I guess."

Maybe. But here's what I think: The right time will never come if you're never ready for it.

More than two millennia ago, a philosopher and politician named Seneca living in ancient Rome observed, "Luck is what happens when preparation meets opportunity." No one has ever proved him wrong, and the same idea echoes through the ages. It was Thomas Jefferson who once quipped, "I'm a great believer in luck, and I find the harder I work, the more I have of it." The American inventor Thomas Edison suggested, "Opportunity is missed by most people because it is dressed in overalls and looks like work." Or, as Malcolm Gladwell would probably put it, luck happens to those who put in the hours.

If you're not ready for it when it comes, your luck will always be bad.

When I was just starting out as a public speaker I got my first lucky break. Or so I thought. At that point in my "career," I hadn't gotten much beyond step one—I knew I wanted to be a nationally known speaker and I wanted to jump right in. I hadn't really put in many hours yet because I didn't even realize I should or that I needed to. I thought what I'd chosen to do was easy. Talk to a group of people for maybe an hour and get paid for it? Yes, please. I love talking! I love getting paid! Honestly, I probably thought that was all there was to it.

I'd already landed a few small gigs and was feeling pretty good about myself, but, truth is, I wasn't anyone special. People didn't know me, and most of the people who did were still betting against the pretentious goof-off foster kid. But, against all odds and good sense, a friend of a friend's mom's uncle's second cousin (or something) landed me an interview spot on *Fox and Friends*.

This was the big time: national TV, a huge live audience—I was a kid just starting out and I'd made it. Luck had come my way. I jumped at the opportunity and said yes to the offer.

I shouldn't have.

I loved the idea of live national TV—I dreamed of being a renowned speaker, after all—but I wasn't prepared. I didn't do my research. I didn't know my audience, and I didn't know my own craft. And it showed. I went on live TV before a huge audience and embarrassed the network and absolutely humiliated myself. It was bad enough that none of the other Fox networks would have me on for years. I was sort of blacklisted. In hindsight, I'm just happy this incident happened before YouTube was a thing.

Did I get lucky? Yes. Was I ready for it? No. My dream had come true—I'd landed in the spotlight on the national stage before a live audience—and it turned into a nightmare because I wasn't ready. I hadn't refined my dream and I hadn't put in the hours.

Are you ready to succeed?

Ask yourself, honestly, "Am I ready?" If given the shot tomorrow, could you make it? Is this your fight to win?

Given the opportunity, will you humiliate yourself, or will you flourish?

MAKING THE JUMP

All right, the time has come. Get out there. Put your hands on the wheel and see how she drives. If you're still in love with the car, it's time to make a purchase.

But the only way you'll ever know is if you get behind the wheel.

Who are the first three people you are going to pursue? What do you know about them already? If you could have ten uninterrupted minutes alone with them, what would you ask? Be sure to be prepared. Know what you want to know. Know whom to talk to.

Time to kick the tires.

TALES OF THE JUMP

Abbie Cobb has wanted to act since she was a little girl. She wasn't always sure she could make money at it, but as she grew up, she educated herself as much as possible on what it would take to make acting a career. She read books, took classes, and trained at home. She also learned the art of working *survival jobs,* those jobs you take in order to stay independent. Abbie knew that to pursue her real goals, she needed income to pay the bills and pay for training. She worked as a nanny, office assistant, and an extra. She even took a gig playing Tinkerbell on Hollywood Boulevard.

Abbie didn't know if she wanted to act in film, television, or onstage, but she knew that she loved to act. Eventually, Abbie got her break, and she has had recurring roles on *90210* and *Suburgatory.*

You knew from the beginning what you wanted to do. Was there ever a moment when you realized that you could actually go for it? That you didn't need the survival job anymore? That it was time to fully devote yourself to acting?

I was actually at the house where I was a nanny. It was a nightmare job. I came home crying almost every day. While I was working there, I told the mother, my boss, that I had a few small acting jobs and was starting to get more auditions. I had already told her that she might need to find a sub or a backup nanny to transition me out; I could sense I was getting busier, and so she was already in the process of trying to find someone else. I got a phone call that I'd booked a recurring role on *90210,* and I knew I wouldn't be available anymore. It ended up being perfect timing, where she had just found someone else to start as a trial when I got this job. I asked if it was possible to be done tomorrow, and she said yes. So I went home and cried from happiness and never went back.

Were there moments when you wanted to give up? What kind of resistance did you encounter—external or internal—to actually sticking with this dream?

I'm just sort of a crazy passionate person, and I'm really, really assertive. Too assertive for my own good sometimes. It never really entered my mind that it wasn't going to happen. It was just a matter of *when.* So the frustration came not from "I'm never going to be able to do what I want to do" but from "I want to do it now. Why do I have to wait? Why do I have to dress up as Minnie Mouse and host this birthday party where I'm getting spit on and kicked and coming home covered in sticky juice?" I wanted to be making art. I wanted to be doing projects that matter. My frustration came from wrestling with patience. It didn't seem fair that some people—because they knew someone or because they had the right agent—were able to do the work that I desperately wanted to do and felt I could handle.

You said that when you were a kid, you knew you wanted to be an actor. Where did that dream start?

When I was little, I would watch certain movies over and over. One of the VHS tapes that I was constantly watching was a

Shirley Temple marathon that my mom had recorded for me. It was three or four movies. I would watch them over and over again. I knew that she was little and that she was acting and that that was her job. I specifically remember talking with my dad, and I asked him—I was eight—if I could be a movie star if I wanted to be. He said, "Well, yeah!" I said, "Could I be one right now?" He said, "Sure, I guess!" I thought it was so cool. I took him literally and thought "I'll do it tomorrow!"

When you were considering a career in acting, what sort of research did you do to figure out if this was really what you wanted to do?
A lot. I actually spent a lot of time and money and careful planning to make sure this was a wise decision. I first pursued a degree in college. A lot of people come out to Los Angeles with stars in their eyes because they're movie buffs. They have nothing on their résumé, they don't have an agent, and they don't know the difference between an agent and manager. They just show up on Hollywood Boulevard and want to know where the actors hang out.

I really took extreme measures to make sure I wasn't going to make those mistakes. So I pursued a degree in theater first, which helped educate me on what part of the country I needed to be in—New York or Chicago or Los Angeles. I invested my summers in plays to expand my résumé. I spent a lot of money to go to showcases and conventions that were national competitions, with national talent and panels of VIPs that were managers from New York City and presidents of major film companies and agents for famous actors. I took notebooks full of notes from all these seminars and workshops. I took great lengths to find out as much as I could about the professional industry, including completing a four-year degree.

From there, I took a test run in Los Angeles for three

months, working with an agent, making sure that Los Angeles was even a place where I wanted to live. I offered myself as a free intern to learn more. I was willing to take a survival job that was inconvenient and humbling, being one of 1,400 background players that were being herded around like cattle. It was an opportunity to learn. I feel like I did whatever I could to prepare myself. I knew if I didn't like any of those things, I had time to switch my major or get a secondary degree. I could go into teaching. I didn't want to waste time by jumping in if I wasn't ready or wasn't sure that it was what I was meant to do.

When you did the test run in Los Angeles, what was the experience like? What did it teach you about what to expect from this career?
I went to a conference while I was still in college. An agent offered to work with me, but she said I needed to be in Los Angeles. After school let out a few months later, I planned to spend the whole summer in Los Angeles. I found a place to live for just a few months. I didn't know what to expect, but I had enough money where I wouldn't have to work a survival job for those three months. Any jobs that I did find would be a bonus. So I got there and met with her in her office. I asked her if I could intern in her office. She said yes, but that she couldn't pay. But, of course, I was more than welcome to work for free. So every Tuesday and Thursday, I worked in her office and found out about background acting. Every other day of the week, I tried out background acting or working as an "extra." I subscribed to all kinds of magazines and newspapers and saw a casting notice for a play. In the evenings I would go to rehearsals for this play.

So I filled my whole time for three months figuring out if I liked it. I filled it with behind-the-scenes office work, where I observed all these actors sending this agent their headshots. Which ones stand out, and why? What makes my agent crazy?

What do actors do that agents hate? I learned all this from the production-office side. Then I was Girl #36 on a TV show. I also did theater to experience every side of Los Angeles that I was able to. I made a little bit of money, which was nice. By the end of the summer, I was able to evaluate: Was I able to make money? Which avenue did I like: set or office or theater? I realized I liked it all and wanted it all. I could see myself living in Los Angeles. Not only had I become comfortable with the idea of being there professionally but also I had been living in the city and learned the roads, traffic, weather, safe neighborhoods, how much things cost, etcetera. I familiarized myself with the community, not just the professional avenue that I was pursuing.

When you met with people who had the jobs you wanted, what kinds of questions did you ask? What was some of the best advice you received?

Like I said, I pursued this really hard and am assertive to a fault. I tried my best to find answers to my questions—and I really couldn't, which disappointed me in a lot of ways. I went to school for this, and I felt like I didn't have the proper training, and didn't have anyone I could ask questions to that knew the answers. What makes a good headshot? How do I attach my headshot to my résumé? Really basic things I didn't learn in school, which disappointed me. I wish I'd had better help, which is why I've made a concerted effort since to provide answers to young actors I meet.

I made mistakes, read a bunch of books. Some things were helpful and some things weren't addressed at all. So I eventually wrote my own book. I wanted to become a mentor because I really didn't have anybody in my situation. I had questions about combining performance and personal faith. What does that look like? Is it okay? I couldn't find a book about being in Los Angeles and being a person of faith. I had so many questions without anyone to ask. So I sort of created my own resource for people who, hopefully, come behind me and can get answers to their questions.

After your test run when you were getting ready to actually go for it, what sort of game plan did you go in with?
I worked a lot while preparing to make my move, so I had some savings. That was important just in case I didn't start working right away. I kept in touch with my contacts while I was away from Los Angeles; my agent had agreed to continue to work with me when I returned. I spent a week apartment hunting in the neighborhoods I had already scoped out. I bought resources I needed, like a laptop and a Not for Tourists guide to the city. I had those things with me to help me practically. I knew what kind of a job I needed, even though I didn't know the specific job. Then I dove in after finding an apartment. I had a meeting with my agent my first week back in Los Angeles. After that, I started to look for auditions and for a survival job.

What kind of support structure did you have going in? How important were other people helping you in this journey?
My parents were supportive. My agent in Los Angeles encouraged me to come out and told me it was possible. She was honest with me about how much money I could make, etcetera. I had a lot of people in the industry from showcases and conventions saying, "Yes, you need to be in this business. I think you are someone who can make it. You need to pursue it while you can." I had affirmation from industry professionals that I didn't just have stars in my eyes. I had a place in my craft and I had something to share and it was good.

What kind of setbacks did you encounter? How did you deal with them?

I prepared for the struggle of becoming a professional working actor, so it didn't feel like a struggle at the time. But every time you audition and don't get it, or you work really hard for a role and they tell you it's not right for you, or you work background on the show and see who is cast, there's a feeling of injustice rising up in you because the chosen actors are flippant with their careers and treat people badly. You think, "I could do that, but not treat people that way. I'm not getting a chance to do that and this person is wasting a gift they've been given." It's not a setback, but it helped shape my perspective. I value my time in background work. Now when I'm on set, I treat people with respect. I know what it's like to be an extra, so I treat the extras with respect. I treat production assistants with respect. I'm thankful for those unpleasant experiences because it makes me appreciate what I have now. I was also watching people drop out of this industry left and right. People who hadn't prepared and had just come off the bus; they were like, "Why can't I get an agent? Why can't I get into the union? This isn't fair!" They took rejection hard and didn't pursue a survival job and didn't have a lot of savings. They experienced setback after setback because they hadn't put in the work before diving in.

When did you feel like you'd arrived?

My first job ever was for a Disney Channel movie called *Starstruck,* which was two and a half years into my experience. I still had my survival job, but I booked this movie and I worked it out so I could do both. I remember I had worked as an extra on other Disney shows, and I was given the instructions to go to the Disney lot for my table read for the movie. I had to enter through the same gate as I did for the other shows. This time I was working as a regular cast member and had a parking spot. I walked in and showed my ID to the guard, and I walked to the lot and knew exactly where I was going because it's the same office where extras wait until they're needed for other shows. So I sat down at a big long table and everybody had an assigned seat and a script with their name on it. I sat down and realized these were the same chairs I had sat in so many times. But this time I was sitting in them and would have my own stand-in and have my own trailer. That moment was "Finally! This is a real job."

The second experience was leaving that nanny job. I got to my car and cried, overwhelmed with happiness. I knew I would never have to go back into that house because I finally didn't need it anymore. I knew I was going to be paid to do what I loved.

Very recently, on a TV show I did, I went to my trailer and checked in and got ready and the call for me came to go to wait in the "video village," where the cast sits. I'd always had a chair that said CAST on it. But I went over there and had a chair with my name on it! I froze and my eyes filled with tears. I couldn't believe it. I'd been working for three years and I'd never had a chair with my actual name on it. When I was little, I thought that would be when I knew I had made it. When I was a little girl, all I wanted was to sit in a chair that had my name on the back of it. I was so excited. I took a picture of it and sent it to my mom.

You're now a working actress. You've come a long way in the last few years. What are your dreams now?

I'm living my dream. This is all I ever wanted: to be paid to do what I love and do what I knew I was born to do. I feel like I'm fulfilling those things that drive me. I don't pay much attention to the future because I'm focused right now on sustaining my dream. My dream is to be able to continue to do this. I know long careers have ups and downs and I want to do what I can to make mine sustainable. Some people have a dream of only doing big feature films, and that would be fun, but I really love my jobs. I'm fine just working in television forever or doing a stint on Broadway that television credits might allow me to do. Actually, that would be really great. My whole life I wanted to do Broadway in New York City, so I'd love to do that at some point and nod to my early dream in that way. Basically, my dream now is avoiding going backward. I just want to keep moving forward.

Step Four: Choose Your Dream-Job Path

It's decided. After exploring all possibilities, refining your options, and taking the top contenders for a test-drive in the real world, you know exactly what dream job to jump for. The Z factor is locked and loaded.

Time to figure out how to get there.

But before we get to the actual planning part, you have one more very important decision to make. You see, in most cases, there are (at least) two paths toward your dream job:

1. The Entrepreneurial Path

2. The Career Path

If you were paying attention earlier in this book I already revealed my bias, but I'll show my hand again:

I think you should take path number two.

That might surprise you, coming from me. If you know anything about me (and, by this time, you should), you'll know that I chose path number one. You'll also know that everything worked out pretty great. So . . . why would I recommend that you do the opposite?

I'm glad you asked.

If you're leaning toward striking out on your own, we need to have a talk. As an entrepreneur myself, there are a few misconceptions to address before you kiss corporate employment goodbye and dive into starting your own business.

First, there's no such thing as working for yourself. Hate to break it to you, but you will always work for other people. Even if you're the boss or the only person in your company, you're still working for other people—your customers, your clients, your audience, or even your employees. It's important not to forget that, because if you ignore everybody else, you're never going to make any money.

You will always have a boss. There will always be demands on your life, and someone or something breathing down your neck. Deadlines still need to be met. Bills still need to be paid. You will still have responsibilities, only now you'll feel *more* pressure. You'll always be answering to somebody. All you've done now by striking out on your own is raised the stakes.

Second, entrepreneurship isn't necessarily easier than working for a company, doesn't necessarily pay more, and isn't the only way to make a living doing what you love. Most of the time it's harder and, especially at first, usually pays less. Most new businesses fail. *Most fail*. More than half. The odds for you on path number one really aren't all that good.

Furthermore, path number one is often unnecessary. Many people assume the only way they'll ever get to do what they really want to do is by working for themselves. Usually, these people are wrong. Let's go back for a second to presenting versus real problems (remember life lesson number two?). For people determined to venture out on their own, the real problem is often one of control. They want to have it—or else they're just disagreeable people who don't like having to answer to other people for their decisions. I'll tell you right now, owning your own business will *not* make those problems go away. In fact, they'll probably make them worse.

Go back to your motives for a second and ask yourself again why one path appeals to you more than another. Is it because it presents you with freedom to do the kind of work you love? Or is it because you're resistant to ceding control of a part of your life?

If it's possible to take path number two, take it.

This may come as a surprise, but it's usually possible to get your dream job by—wait for it—keeping your day job. A job with income gives you flexibility. It lets you say no without having to obsess over the consequences, and it lets you say yes only when the opportunity is right. Otherwise, all you're really concerned about is getting paid. Keeping your job gives you more creative freedom.

DO THIS STEP OR ELSE

What you choose in step four radically affects steps five, six, and seven. The difference between becoming CEO of an established company and starting your own company is vast indeed, as is the difference between, say, working as a chef and owning your own restaurant.

Sometimes, depending on what your specific dream is, this choice is easy. If you want to work for Apple, you're going to have to choose path number two—you can't start your own company called Apple and say it's the same thing. The lawyers would eat you alive.

At the same time, however, there are plenty of stories of people who started off on path number one and created their own company/product/service in a market related to company X, and, eventually, it became so awesome and successful on its own that company X bought it. Now these people technically work for company X and they're on path number two. So it can be complicated.

You have to be realistic about where you want to end up: (1) working for yourself, or (2) working for a company. But it's even more important that you're realistic about where you want to start and what you're getting into.

WHY YOU'LL SETTLE

If you have the entrepreneurial itch, maybe you'll want to get started right away. To you I say, moving quickly can be an advantage, of course—if you're moving in the right direction. What I want you to do before you start laying your plans and implementing them is to count the cost. Starting a company isn't a game and isn't necessarily fun. You could wreck a lot of relationships and lose a lot of money if you jump in unprepared.

Others of you may also have the entrepreneurial itch, the irrepressible deep desire to strike out on path number one, but you're leaning toward path number two—for the wrong reasons: not because it's probably smarter, but because it seems safer, and because you're secretly hoping "something happens" on path number two that makes it "impossible" to take path number one in the future "like you planned." You're looking for an excuse to bail.

Question your motives, people. Be truthful with yourself.

SHAKE IT UP

Honestly evaluate the advantages of both paths—and then choose. Perhaps an illustration will help. Say that, like Sue Fletcher, whom we heard from earlier, you love to bake. You make muffins and cupcakes and cookies and tarts and all sorts of things just for fun, and people are always telling you that you should open a bakery. You really are a good baker, and it's highly likely people would pay to eat your confections. In fact, you've had colleagues at work hire you to make birthday cakes before.

You're pretty sure you do, in fact, want to be a baker. You've defined and refined your plan, you've test-driven it by working for a bakery, and the work, the hours, the emotional rewards—they all appeal to you. This has become your dream. So, which path do you choose?

Path Number One—The Entrepreneurial Path

Paul Graham, one of the founders of noted start-up funding resource Y Combinator, believes that people were never meant to have a boss. He suggests, "It will always suck to work for large organizations, and the larger the organization, the more it will suck." Several studies seem to support his conclusions. I read once that 89 percent of freelancers report being happier since beginning freelancing. And, let's be honest, entrepreneurship has worked out really well for one person you know: me. I absolutely love being my own CEO. Then again, I've always been excited about running a business—most people aren't.

People who aren't excited about running a business should never, ever take path number one, because it requires you to *run a business*. Even if you're a business of one, you're still a business. If our baker friend chooses path number one, she may get to bake. She may get to bake a lot, in fact, especially if, at first, she's doing all of it alone. But she also has to rent and maintain a Web site or storefront, balance the books, take orders, make deliveries, and obtain proper licensure and certifications for selling consumables. Sadly, at the end of the day, most of what she will end up doing isn't baking at all.

Path Number Two—The Career Path

If our friend chooses path number two, she'll bake a lot. In fact, that could be all she ever does. She could find the best bakery in town and work there as head baker all the days of her life and never have to lift a finger to handle the tasks of making sure the bills are paid and the dough is ordered and floors are mopped at the end of the night. Not her problem.

Maybe in the midst of all that, she realizes she's actually interested in the bookkeeping and management of a business. She's around it all the time and has picked up on a lot. She knows what it takes to run a business because she's worked in one for a while and learned the ropes. It's just possible she'll consider opening her own bakery now. And if she does, she's in a much better position to do it now.

This is your choice.

POSSIBLE HURDLES

Now, if you haven't already figured it out, there's a big difference between someone who enjoys baking and someone who wants to be a baker or open a bakery. Someone can love baking, but does that mean they will be successful doing it for a living? Maybe, maybe not. Just because you love baking does not mean you have the ability to deal with everything that working at it for a living requires.

The hard truth is this: Before you jump, you need to have a sense of what your dream job is going to really entail. This is the hard work of step three—test-driving your dream. If you do your due diligence in step three, you'll know what it takes to make your dream job happen. You'll know that you might not be ready (yet) for the entrepreneurial, but you are ready for the career path—in our example, to jump headfirst into your love of baking. It's all about knowing the difference between doing something you love—and biting off more than you can chew.

Knowing the difference is invaluable.

The problem, ironically, is not that you might be afraid to jump—it's that you might jump too soon. The mistake people often make is trying to turn their hobby into a dream job overnight—only to find out that what they love has turned into something they hate. Don't get me wrong, there are those people who jump headfirst into path number one and succeed. Trust me, I did it. But that's not the path for everyone—nor is it necessarily the most beneficial path.

There's another reason why it's worthwhile to work for someone else first before going out on your own. If you jump out on your own, you're, well, on your own. You're facing circumstances and situations you never thought existed, having to make decisions on the fly—decisions that have real ramifications. Look at it this way: If you work for someone else in the beginning, it's like having a multiyear internship—and getting paid for it.

You can develop partnerships, build your network, and gain invaluable experience facing those circumstances and situations alongside someone who has been down that road before. You get the benefit of watching someone else make the decisions and learning from them.

Here's something else that happens. You get to learn about the business without investing your own money into it. In other words, you get to learn about the business on someone else's dime. Now, down the road a bit, it may be a different story. After you've learned the business and built your network, you'll be in a better position to decide whether you want to get out on your own, and you can launch your business with the experience gained working for someone else.

MAKING THE JUMP

So it all comes down to this: Which path will you take? Path number one? Or path number two? Will you be working for yourself or for others?

I said it before, but it's worth restating: You will always have a boss. Even if you "make it." In fact, I would argue *especially* if you make it. Because if you make it—whatever that means for you and your dream job—then you'll have a lot more people to take care of to keep the engines running. Customers. Clients. Employees.

If you think that by taking path number one you'll never have to work for anyone again—think again. You're kidding yourself. Check your motivation—and be truthful.

Sure, path number one will offer you more control, but path number two will offer you less responsibility and greater financial flexibility. While path number one is like jumping into the deep end, path number two is a gradual immersion, wading in the shallow end for a while and then moving into deeper waters only if you want to.

Now, let me talk to those of you bent toward path number one. If you do have that entrepreneurial itch, it isn't ever going to go away. It will haunt you for the rest of your life. You'll wake up in the middle of the night thinking about it. So, you can try and stifle it and live your life in a constant irritation because you're not doing what you know you were made to do, or you can start scratching.

The choice is yours.

TALES OF THE JUMP

As described on theartofvision.com, Erik Wahl recounts his story:

> At an early age, a well-meaning teacher told Erik Wahl that "art is not your strength." Being a disciplined student, Erik

listened. He put down his crayons and paintbrushes and didn't pick them up again for another twenty years. In the meantime, he studied hard and learned to play by the rules. Erik concluded, like most, that strong grades, a solid college education, and a good corporate job with predictable growth would be sufficient.

But after ten years in the corporate world, Erik could sense his talents were wasting away. However, it wasn't until he lost everything that he found himself.

Fearlessly determined to break through the system, Erik and his wife, Tasha, created the Art of Vision, a company capable of "setting the captives of corporate America free" from the same robotic, mind-numbing path to which he had previously fallen prey.

What did you used to do?
I previously had an appropriately professional job as a partner in an entertainment agency. It was a decent job by most standards.

What did you want to do?
When I first started work out of college, I wanted security. I wanted to find a stable career with good opportunities for climbing the ladder of success.

What was it that made you realize it was time for a change?
I wish I could tell you it was a valiant, bold decision, but it was anything but. It was gut-wrenching. I lost everything in the process—everything that had been taught to me about what it meant to be successful. It was like a shark attack. I was married and had three boys under the age of four, and what I thought it meant to be a man and to provide stability for my family exploded. I was addicted to security, to prestige and possessions,

and when this security was taken away, I panicked. Everything I knew about actualizing the American Dream was wiped out, and I was going to need to start from ground zero. It tormented me at night. I'd lay awake thinking about all of the losses that questioning my path had caused.

A friend of mine who was a behavioral psychologist was watching me crash and burn. He recommended that I find a cathartic release. Maybe something that gave me joy as a child.

I started to paint. I found solace and began to paint with reckless abandon. I had no formal training, but I found it therapeutic to spread paint on canvas, to express my discontent and even explore what I thought real happiness might look like. I started to hang out with local artists. I studied art history and artistic technique. I was intoxicated by art and began to see it not only as a noun (a finished piece of work) but also as a verb (an engaged, passionate way of viewing the world).

I spent all my spare time with artists, but what I found was a sort of disconnect. The artists had incredible vision and insight into the world around us, but no practical application. They couldn't translate art into a living, and they were frustrated. Some became self-absorbed and dark. That whole starving-artist cliché was true.

That's when I had my epiphany. I had been seduced into a life of mediocrity. I had been lulled to sleep by this linear, predictable life of safety. I had buried my talents and my potential in exchange for solid ground. So I staged a full-scale rebellion. I wrote an entire thesis in one night.

What if I combined the creativity and perspective of an artist with the business strategies that I had studied and experienced? I began to research the psychology of performance. I poured myself into this concept the same way I did with art, and I stumbled onto something amazing.

There was a pattern to visionary excellence. The artists who create innovative works of art (the Picassos, the Mozarts and Beethovens) are exactly the same as the game-changing entrepreneurs (the Zuckerbergs, Bransons, and Disneys). They use similar visions to create business empires their competitors never think possible. They create products their customers don't even know they want.

I continued to paint, sculpt, write, and create, but I also began to develop a presentation to share with audiences. I wanted it to be as much entertainment as informational. What if I painted to live music while I shared this breakthrough idea? I dove into the world of performing.

I had nothing left to lose by pouring myself into this new adventure. The message was compelling, the delivery entertaining. Audiences loved the unconventional style of delivery, and my new career exploded. I got the privilege of performing at a few national conferences, and it was like hitting the lotto. The business has grown exponentially every year because I had discovered something and was doing something no one else had done before.

What initially kept you from pursuing your dream job? What resistance—external or internal—did you face?
Linear thinking and an addiction to safety were the biggest things holding me back.

After cycling through the refining and test stages, what path did you choose to pursue your dream career?
I decided to study the great entertainers. Traditional speakers who lectured behind the podium bored me. I wanted to study Jay-Z, Bono, Jerry Seinfeld, deadmau5, Mick Jagger, and others

to learn how they engaged an audience. There was a cadence and timing and rhythm that was captivating, and that's what I built my presentation upon.

Do you wish you'd done things differently?
In retrospect, I needed my midlife crisis to actualize this dream. If I had been formally trained as an artist, I would have been taught logically how to paint. Instead, I taught myself to draw passionately, to entertain with passion, and to operate my business with passion. I wish I would have discovered this treasure earlier, but since I didn't, my goal is to share my story with audiences. To give them permission to break free from conventional lives and take a risk to live with passion.

Step Five: Create Your Dream-Job Plan

It's time to lay out the grand plan for achieving your dream job! Ready?

Dream It and Do It!!!
Congratulations! You've just received the worst advice ever!

Seriously, this is pretty much the least valuable piece of guidance I've ever heard, and it is issued with emotional intensity by just about every motivational speaker out there. If you really want to drive yourself crazy, just follow this advice. Anything or anyone who tells you to do this is either a shameless huckster or lives in a quaint little fairy-tale land.

In the Disney-movie version of your life, your dream arrives on a silver platter, maybe after a few catchy songs are sung. Disney has a lot to account for: They may be the only company to simultaneously raise the expectations of an entire generation and lower what is required from them.

So what is really required from you? Well, to make your dreams come true, you actually have to take a step forward and do something. As much as we'd love to hear that all we need to do is "dream" our future, it's going to take more than merely dreaming—it's going to take a healthy dose of doing.

So why do we still use terms like "dream job"? Easy. Because we still have dreams. As silly as it may sound to define something as a "dream job," we really do fantasize about what our lives could be like if we were to do this or quit that. Most of us probably don't break out into song or dance with animals, but, hey, to each his own.

We have this deep internal belief that things—in our own life, in the world—can be better. We can't ignore the image in our head of what our perfect "dreamlike" life would look like. We are all fully capable of imagining our days filled with activities that bring us life instead of sucking it out of us. So, while it may seem a little silly to sing about a dream, it's a completely different matter when you learn how to define the dream. Because if you can define the dream, then you have something to shoot for—something to take positive steps toward. In short, the dream now has a path to become a reality in your life.

So forget about the Disney version of realizing your dream. Here's the Cinderella story, Shipp-style:

- Quit sitting around in your evil stepmom's house.
- Get a haircut. If necessary, hire some cute cartoon animals to make you clothes.
- Learn more about yourself so you can determine who you'd like to date.
- Make necessary changes in your own behavior that will make you more appealing in a relationship.
- Go to the ball. In fact, go to as many balls as you can. Make yourself available to others.
- Learn to say no when the wrong dude comes along.

- Recognize the prince when he arrives.
- Live happily ever after.

Disney dreams are for sleeping people. What you need to do is wake up. If you are vague about your dream job, or just simply hope to "luck" into it one day, that's all it will ever be—a dream.

If you're serious about seeing your dream become a reality, here's what it will really take:

> Dream it: This is where you start—dreaming big. But
>   don't stop here, there's more . . .
> Document it: Write your dream down; be specific.
> Define it: Refine, refine, refine. Go all out researching.
>   Kick the tires.
> Do it: Get after it. Take positive steps toward the goal of
>   making your dream a reality.

Here we are, at that final stage. After documenting and defining the specific things you need to do to make this dream happen, it's time to create the plan and move forward.

DO THIS STEP OR ELSE

The past four steps have all been about discovering and refining your dream. Every step along the way has been geared toward turning your dream into a practical reality. Now, it's time to devise your plan—and pursue it with all you have. This is the hard work that will make your dream job a reality.

Until now, this has been an idea—something you've been weighing and talking about with others around you. But now that you've made it to step five, it's time to plot your course of action.

Now that you've written down the dream and refined it again and again, I want you to think about the next three actions you need to take.

That's it. Not what you're going to do for the rest of your life or even, necessarily, for the rest of the month. Honestly ask yourself: "What are the next three things I need to do to bring my dream into reality?" Write them down as part of your plan. This leaves room for both continual editing as well as focus on small, manageable goals. If you want to start making films, don't spend your time thinking about your Oscar acceptance speech. Focus your energy on that first script, first page, or first concept. This is where the journey begins. This is how you make the dream happen. *What are the next three steps you need to take?*

Remember, success is not a single act. It is a compilation of many single acts moving in the same direction. There is a lot of power in creating easy goals and consistently meeting them. Even if it's just one action item, complete it and come up with a new one. Eventually, you'll make it to the Oscar acceptance speech—three action steps at a time. In the meantime, be focused, be patient, and, above all else, be relentless.

WHY YOU'LL SETTLE

One of the biggest reasons you'll settle is the temptation to look at where your role models are now. We talked about this in step three. If you compare yourself to industry experts like Bono or Stephen King or Warren Buffett, you're right: You should give up. There is no way you can compete with them. But if you compare yourself to Bono when he began as a little Irishman who admitted he had a terrible singing voice in a lower-class Irish garage, it will give you hope for the future of your dream.

Another failure to move forward will come from your desire to double- and triple- and quadruple-check everything to "make sure" you're prepared. Really, you're just having control issues. Trust me. I've been there. On the one hand, patience is important; quitting before you have something to quit for and a way to pay the bills is hasty. But if you keep biding your time waiting for the perfect moment, you'll never jump. This is why we need to focus on 3 steps instead of the giant blueprint. If you can't do the first 3 things, you'll never complete all 115 things that will be required of you in the long run.

The last thing is patience. It's okay to wait for the right moment. Remember when I said, "Don't quit your day job"? It's true—but also don't wait forever. You know how some people tend to always talk about quitting but never do? The job may have been awesome at one point—it may have even been their dream job—but somewhere along the line they settled. They became unhappy and couldn't bring themselves to do anything about it. Then it was too late. They found themselves in a rut, paralyzed by fear, unable to move forward. Don't let that be *you*.

SHAKE IT UP

I can't say for sure how YOU are going to need to shake up your plan. This book is for people who want to land a job at their dream company, or start their own photography business, or become an actress, or start the best coffee shop on the planet, or start a nonprofit. Everybody's first three actions are going to be different. So one of the best things I can suggest is to revisit something you put together in step three, the list of people you want to pursue, people whom you sought out for their expertise and who have already expressed interest in your venture. Listen to them first when it comes to the next three steps. Your dream is going to require very specific actions, and I don't want to give you a bunch of vague advice. Listen to those who have been there.

That said, there are a few common obstacles that I can warn against that go for just about any new venture you are planning on.

POSSIBLE HURDLES

The first and easiest hurdle to solve is not being specific about your plan. If you find yourself saying, "I don't need to write it down! My dream lives inside of me!" you're wrong. Write your plan down and write down your first three action points. Keep these in front of you every day. Revisit them often. Ask yourself: "What have I done today to move forward in making my dream a reality?" Without this kind of relentless pursuit, your dream is in jeopardy.

Next, if you're considering any major investment in the name of pursuing your dream—say, in clothes or equipment or software—act with caution. Professional equipment doesn't make you a professional. You can make a name for yourself as a photographer with the camera on your iPhone. You don't need fancy business cards or the newest computer. You don't need a fancy suit to impress people.

Third, avoid the crowds. Tried and true is often dangerously overtrodden. Want to be exceptional at what you do? Overestimate your competition and underestimate your chances—you'll have a much better shot at succeeding. In the famous book *Blue Ocean Strategy,* Renée Mauborgne and W. Chan Kim argue that if you are starting something new—and want to be successful— you need to avoid the "red water" filled with chum, because chum attracts a feeding frenzy. Everyone who is looking for an easy meal is attracted to this area because it's simple. But if you want to create something new, something attractive and long- lasting, you need to avoid the chum-filled red ocean and look for the blue ocean—where everything is clear and you have separated yourself from those who are looking for an easy meal. It will be harder to find a meal, but you won't have to compete with those who are looking for an easy out. Success may not come instantly, but it will be much more rewarding—and come with a bigger payoff.

Fourth, you might get tripped up over finances. Always budget wisely ahead of time, because not having the money is one of the easiest excuses for not making any progress. Too many people end up saying, "When I get the cash, I will . . ." or, "When I can save enough to quit this job, I will . . ." The sad fact is that this rarely happens. Your action step in this case should be to save money, not plan on how to use the money once you have it. Stay dedicated to the action right in front of you.

The last hurdle, which I can't put enough stress on, is the need for accountability. This may include a mentor you discovered in step three, but it may also include some really great friends who are desperate for you to succeed. You need to share your dream with them, share your first three action steps, and give them permission to kick your butt if you are not sticking to your plan. If you want to watch your dream die, the best way is to keep it a secret. This is your opportunity to make it public. It's a doorway that you can't walk back through. This may sound weird, but create an environment where you will actually feel uncomfortable around your friends and family if you are unable to make those next three steps come true. This is your moment, your inciting incident that you can't undo. This will be one of your greatest motivators to make sure you clear all the hurdles on the way to your dream job.

MAKING THE JUMP

Let's be honest. This step describes the kind of work it takes to succeed. No more empty fantasies. This is the hard work that isn't sexy or glamorous but that will get you to your dream job. This is also the place where most people make excuses and bail. Whether they leave things to chance or don't do their homework, the fact of the matter is this: They quit. Don't be one of those people. This is the place where you need to press through and do the work necessary to make your dream happen. This is the time to do a gut check. Do you really want this or not? Are you willing to do what it takes to succeed? If you've made it this far in the book, I think you are.

To keep from bailing out, you have to know exactly where you are in this process. You've written down your dream. You've done the refining work. You've done the research to know what the dream looks like and what it takes to get there. You've even taken the dream for a test-drive. Now, you need to find a way to measure your strategy—in order to see the progress and to keep you on course.

Here's one thing to do. Make a checklist of all the skill sets you need to acquire. What time, energy, and resources will you need to invest? Calculate the amount of time you think it will take. And don't forget your three action points—what are the next three things you need to do. Keep a running list of these action points. You'll be able to track the progress you're making.

Always, always be specific. If you're vague about the plan to fulfill your dream job, it will only remain a dream. If you can't be specific with the plan and the next three action points, your dream is going to end shipwrecked off some deserted island along the way. The only way your dream will come true is by planning out your steps and working that plan.

You see, here's the thing: Passion without direction won't work. You can have all the passion in the world, but if you don't have some specific steps to take, forget it. You might as well move on with your so-called life. You need direction. You need a plan. You need to identify the steps you're going to take and then—get ready for it—do them.

The time for excuses is over. The time to "wait and see" is over. If you're going to live the dream you've always wanted, it's going to take action. It's going to take you getting off the couch and putting together a plan. Because success only comes from combining passion with action.

And one last thing. When you're putting together your plan, be sure to leave room for the unexpected. This is why you only focus on the next three steps in front you. You might find that after those three steps, the next three may be ones you never thought of. Stay committed to the three action steps right in front of you; then, after that, replenish with the next three action steps, and then the next three.

Ready? Let's get after it!

What are the next three things you need to do?

TALES OF THE JUMP

When Mindy Green was born in 1977, she was diagnosed with a congenital heart defect. At the time, her doctors didn't think she would live more than two years.

But advances in fighting those defects were being made, and her family searched far and wide for doctors who could help. Eventually, they found one, a pediatric cardiologist in Northern California who thought she stood a chance. Mindy was one of the first people in the United States to undergo a groundbreaking treatment. Even then, no one knew how long she would survive. Mindy is now thirty-five years old, and her heart appears to be in perfect condition.

Her early experience with the practice of medicine instilled in her a desire to become a doctor one day. Mindy was a straight-A student and entered the premed program at the University of

California-Santa Barbara. She breezed through her undergraduate years. Then, in her junior year, she got cold feet. She was worried about taking the MCAT, the horrendously difficult test that would allow her entrance to medical school.

Mindy still loved medicine, so she chose to become a physical therapist. After earning her bachelor's degree, she enrolled at the University of Southern California in hopes of earning a doctorate in physical therapy. She was breezing through that program as well.

But something nagged at Mindy.

What was it that made you realize it was time for a change?
I was doing an out-of-town rotation at a children's hospital in Portland. We would have these care meetings once a week, where all the different people and disciplines that cared for the child meet together to review progress and treatment goals. I realized I was more excited and paid more attention to what the doctor was saying—the medical aspect of their treatment. I found myself more interested in overseeing a child's *whole* treatment (which was the role of the team physician) versus being responsible for only one aspect of the treatment (which was the role of the physical therapist). That was when I began thinking I'd made the wrong career choice.

What initially kept you from pursuing your dream job? What resistance, internal or external, did you face?
The biggest resistance was fear. I was scared of failing. I was also scared of making a job change, of all the hard work and long hours that I would face, and of all the additional school debt I would accrue.

I have a vivid memory of driving in my car to see my PT-school girlfriends and wrestling with all the pros and cons of changing my career path. I use the car for thinking and praying and talking to myself a lot. I realized over the summer that despite the intense work-life of being a physician, that was truly what I wanted to do. But here I was, almost graduated as a physical therapist! Going to graduate school cost a lot already, not to mention the time I had invested. I decided, that car ride, that any additional education I had would only add to my ability to treat patients. It may have been costly, but it would make me a better doctor. I couldn't let my past choices continue to stand in the way of my desire to change careers.

When I was younger, my mom used to tell me about how she had become a nurse but always wanted to be a doctor. I remember telling her, when I was about six years old, "Why don't you go back to school now?" But she felt like she couldn't do that. She had three children to raise, a household and ranch to run, and she only had an associate-level degree. But her regret at not becoming a doctor always stuck with me. On that car drive, I thought of my future daughter. I didn't want to tell her, "You can do anything you want" but know that I didn't because I let fear stand in my way. I wanted a different legacy for her. I also realized that I would be in school until I was thirty-one. "Might as well be thirty-one and a doctor," I told my twenty-five-year-old self. I made up my mind to go for it, and I haven't regretted that decision once.

What sort of game plan did you have when you decided to pursue your dream?

I knew I had most of the prerequisites for medical school, but I needed to look into taking the MCAT. Since that test had been such a source of stress, and I was now five to six years past when

I took the core classes tested on the MCAT, I began looking into prep courses.

I also had to decide what to do with my current plan of study. I knew the earliest I could start medical school was in two years. So, I decided to finish the last year of training. I knew it would cost more money, but I believed strongly that it would help me get into medical school, and help make me a better physician. In the meantime, while I waited for my medical school applications to be accepted, I could get a job working with children as a physical therapist. I didn't have a guarantee that I would be accepted that first go-round, and I would need a good job to pay loans!

What steps did you take to prepare for success?
The training course for the MCAT was very important to me. I studied every day, and after four months of working hard, I scored well above my hopes on the actual test.

I worked hard and graduated with honors from PT school. I was actually the valedictorian, which made me very proud.

Additionally, I shadowed our family physician throughout the summer after graduation. This led to an opportunity to go on a medical mission to Haiti, which was an amazing experience.

Lastly, I actually applied to medical school. This required lots of time and research. Each school had its own application, its own essays, and its own requirements. It took quite a while to apply to multiple schools.

What sort of support structure did you have when you set out to pursue your dream?
My parents were very supportive of me accomplishing and achieving my goals. They never made me feel bad about changing my career. Our family physician was also an excellent mentor.

Additionally, throughout the pursuit of my career, I had support from friends and other physicians. My friend turned boy-friend turned husband was also very important to me, especially throughout residency. After my daughter was born partway through my pediatric residency, she became another inspiration to keep going. The theoretical daughter I went back to school for now had a name and a face. When she gets older, I look forward to letting her know how she inspired me even before she was born!

How important were other people to helping you reach your goals?
It is absolutely the support and encouragement of other people that helped me do as well as I did throughout medical school, residency, chief residency and that now help me as a practic-ing physician. True, it is only your hard work and your deter-mination that ultimately result in achieving your goal, but your mentors, family, and friends can certainly give you the fuel to keep going. One example that sticks out in my mind is that after my daughter was born and my maternity leave was over, it was hard to return to the long hours and grueling schedule of residency. I remember telling my program director I wanted to quit. She looked at me and replied, "I will not let you quit."

My mentors gave me encouragement. Their belief in me, their insight, medical knowledge, etcetera, helped shape me into the physician I am today. When I think of the mentors that had the biggest impact on my medical career, it was those who saw something they liked in me and were willing to give their time and effort to see me develop into a great physician. I didn't want to disappoint them or waste their investment in me, so I worked harder.

I had patients that would inspire me with their stories. It is very humbling to have parents trust you to care for their child, so I definitely worked hard to be worthy of that trust.

Lastly, I had the love of my family to get me through. So, in a sense, I couldn't fail.

Step Six: Implement Your Dream-Job Plan

*Whatever you can do, or dream you can, begin it. Boldness
has genius, magic, and power in it. Begin it now.*

—GOETHE

This is where the rubber meets the road. How do you know
you're ready? When you stop dreaming and start doing. When
you believe it. When you've decided to beat fear. When you take
power, instead of waiting for someone to give it to you or hoping
that they'll yield. Don't ask—tell. Or, in the words of Nike,
"JUST DO IT!"

This isn't Tim Ferriss's *The Four-Hour Workweek*. That sounds
nice, and there's no denying his life seems to suit him well. People
were obviously drawn to his message—or at least to the dream
of working 90 percent less.

Here's what I like about the idea: Not having to work, in theory, gives you a lot of freedom. Maybe that's appealing to you,
too. We're suckers for the idea that there's a way to make it without having to do the actual hard work. The other thing is that
Tim focuses on selling consumables in that book—which isn't

even a "dream" for him. It is merely a means to an end, and that
end is freedom from work.

I think that idea misses the whole point of life. If you are
reading this book, it's because you want to take part in or create
your dream, to actually work for something you love. You and I
were made for work. We quite literally would go crazy without
something to do. And rubbing cocoa butter on your belly in a
hammock on some South American beach doesn't qualify, ultimately, as "something to do." If you don't want to put more than
four hours of your time into your work every week, then you
must *hate* your work pretty intensely. The truth is, you need to
stop looking for a shortcut. Why? Because right now your competition is at home working their butts off.

Discipline begets discipline. If you're only working four hours
a week, you're not being disciplined, and your craft will suffer.
You'll lose your edge. Any high school kid with an ounce of discipline will outmaster you in a year, and you will be a has-been,
your overturned hull floating in the ocean as a warning to other
lazy, drifting vessels. You should expect to work—and to work
hard.

I love this quote from one of Hollywood's media darlings,
Ryan Gosling: "The problem with Hollywood is that nobody
works. They have meals. They go to Pilates. But it's not enough.
So they do drugs. If everybody had a pile of rocks in their backyard and spent every day moving them from one side of the yard
to the other, it would be a much happier place."

One of the best things you can do to create discipline in your
work is to create discipline in other areas of your life. This may
sound crazy, but when I started running marathons, which
started taking about two hours a day out of my schedule, I actually became better at my work. And this will really blow your
mind, but when I became a father and had to start disciplining

my time in order to help raise my two children, my work also became more disciplined. Why? It had to! The only way for me to get work done was to be focused when I had the opportunity. Running marathons and raising children have very little to do with being a speaker or writing books or being a TV host, but it has everything to do with focused effort and stamina. As one of my favorite business comics Hugh MacLeod says, "Ninety percent of what separates successful people and failed people is time, effort, and stamina."

This step is about putting in the effort, disciplining yourself to take sustained action in making your dream happen. It's not enough to identify the next three steps you need to take, then putting your feet up and waiting for the phone to ring. It's about taking action—successfully completing the steps you've identified, then uncovering the next three steps you need to take. If you can repeat this over and over again, before you know it, you'll turn around and see the distance you put between who you are now and the person you used to be.

But it begins with a choice.

DO THIS STEP OR ELSE

This is why this implementation step is so important. Because if you don't implement your plan, if you don't continue to move through your three action steps, then the previous five steps mean absolutely nothing. This is the step where you will spend the majority of your life—taking the next three steps, uncovering the next three, and moving forward again. You are focused on the dream, you have refined it, and you figured out the best plan for how to make it happen. But if you don't take the time and effort to continue pursuing and replenishing your three action steps, you will eventually fizzle out.

Frankly, this is the step that separates the men from the boys.

The women from the girls. The gunslingers from the posers. This is where you truly make your mark on society. It's all about your actions.

I mentioned accountability in step five, but it's worth harping on again here in step six. I firmly believe in sharing your dream with everyone who shares a part of your life, because you do not obtain your "dream job" alone. I made a decision early on to surround myself with people who blew me away with their genius. And trust me, brilliant people don't just start appearing out of thin air begging to make your acquaintance. You have to go find them and convince them to spend time with you. I sought out mentors for just about everything in my life. I've got business mentors, spiritual mentors, financial mentors, family mentors, and since I started running marathons, I even have a running mentor.

Why do I surround myself with these people? Honestly, because, if given proper opportunity, I have the potential to make horrible decisions regarding just about everything in my life. But when I surround myself with people whom I care about and whom, somehow, either through small-level threats, bribery, or black magic, I have convinced to care about me, I get the needed push forward, even when I'm too tired to take another step.

I still haven't arrived. I haven't landed that Nobel Prize or mapped out the path to the fountain of youth. I am still fighting, striving in every aspect of my life, to make good decisions for my family, friends, business partners, church, running crew, and just about everyone else who shares my life. These mentors help me in this because I can't do this alone, and, believe me, neither can you.

One of the best things you can create for yourself is an excited and inspiring fan section who will cheer you on every step you take. Surround yourself with people who believe in you and what you are trying to accomplish—who believe in your dream and believe that you are the right person to live that dream. When the tough times come, and they will, you will find that this fan section will help you achieve things you never thought possible.

WHY YOU'LL SETTLE

You're in the midst of your jump now. This is the part where the enemy within will do everything it can to get you to give up and settle back into what is comfortable. It might be the voice inside your head that says you'll never succeed or that you're not good enough or smart enough to make it happen. It might be the thought that the next three steps are just too difficult. It might be the overwhelming desire to put off until tomorrow what you know deep down needs to be done today. It might be the unforeseen setbacks to your plan. Whatever it might be, realize this: The journey to your dream will not be one long success story.

How you view these challenges to your dream—your day-to-day mind-set—will affect whether your plan succeeds or fails. A hopeful, determined mind-set will support your decisions, even when you face setbacks. A pessimistic one will lead you to back down. Your frame of mind is the only thing that will keep you writing the next sentence, making the next call, and meeting with that next person. In order for you to see success, you have to change your mind-set.

SHAKE IT UP

You already know about "self-esteem." I want to introduce a new concept called "step-esteem." Basically, it goes a little something like this: As you go along, you'll find that you experience feelings of success and self-worth in successfully knocking off your steps, one at a time. You gain momentum by fulfilling an action. It's almost as if it were mechanical. It could be as simple as buying that URL you need or knocking out an interview with a professional in your field, or renting an office space, or researching a topic online, or making a sales call. Each little step along the way creates a sense of movement—the little boost you need to keep going.

Don't sweat the big picture. Don't dwell on the past. Just focus on fulfilling your steps and you'll realize that your self-esteem is improving right alongside you step-esteem.

They say that runners are 80 percent more likely to stick to their running plans if they lay their running clothes next to the bed. Runners who do this have little to no option but to step out of bed and into their running shoes. In a way, you can do the same thing with your action steps. Create them the night before and set them out so that when you wake up, the most important part of your day is already planned out.

POSSIBLE HURDLES

You're in the thick of your jump right now, something it may take months to execute, and the hurdles are almost limitless. The closed doors, the perfect URL that someone else has already purchased, the lost investors, the difficult interviews, the unreliable partners—the list goes on and on.

There is no way I can tell you how to deal with each of these hurdles; the list is long. However, what I can tell you to do is to consider your frame of mind. When you're prepared and ready to go, when you've done your homework and know what you want and how to get there, you can handle the challenges that come along. And over time, you will begin to realize that you are becoming a master at knocking out each of those individual steps, which will in turn and over time get you closer and closer to mastering your dream job.

MAKING THE JUMP

Okay, here's the good news. If you've made it this far, you're in good company. You are the few, the brave—those who are moving closer every day to actually living their dream job. While the side of the road is filled with people with good intentions, you are on the road to seeing your dream really happen. Be encouraged.

But also know this: You need to be relentless. Relentless about knocking out each of your individual steps and replenishing them when you do. Implementing your dream isn't easy, but it is the only way to reach the promised land.

With that in mind, there are a few critical things to know if you're going to make it.

You need to learn how to overcome discouragement. No person has ever succeeded without facing challenges. If you think you will avoid challenges, then I want to hear your secret—because it just doesn't happen. Anything that is worth pursuing is going to face obstacles. Nothing comes easy.

Every person who has seen their dream become a reality has had to learn how to deal with failure and setbacks. And this means you, too. The quicker you realize this, the better. Let me be clear here—you are going to fail before you succeed, so just get used to it now.

From my experience, the key to dealing with failure is this: You can't avoid failure and setbacks, but you can control how you react to them. Instead of seeing a setback like the end of the line for your dream, learn from it. See every failure and every setback as an opportunity to learn something about the cost of living your dream job. When you choose to have this mind-set, the fear of failure disappears. I'll go a step further: Failure is necessary. Failure builds within you the mental toughness that you need to succeed. So learn from it. Embrace it.

You'll also need to become the master of what I like to call "the principle of priority." There are a lot of things that will scream for your attention, things that are worthy, things that seem urgent. You can spend all your time doing things that are urgent and never really get around to doing the things that are important. Know the difference and be sure to do the important things first.

Finally, you'll need to surround yourself with other people who are reaching their goals. Nothing will help keep you motivated like seeing someone else doing what it takes to make his or her dream a reality. Think of it as a step-esteem support group. These are your companions, your fellow travelers. These are the people who understand what you are trying to reach and the cost of getting there.

In the end, you need to know one thing. No one—and I mean not a single person—is entitled to their dream. If you want your dream to become a reality, you need to earn it. You need to have what it takes—the willingness to work, the commitment, the dedication—to see it through to the end. You need to press on when you feel like bailing. You need to focus on your goal, and know beyond a shadow of a doubt that you'll eventually reach it.

And, above all else, remember this: An "overnight success" often takes ten years to build. But here's the thing: Is it worth it? Seriously, as you look at your dream on that piece of paper, ask yourself this question: "Is this dream worth all the work I'm going to have to put in?" If you can't answer yes, you've got the wrong dream, and all the effort will be a colossal waste of time.

But if your answer is yes, then you're onto something, something extraordinary. You've found a dream worth pursuing. You've also found the motivation you need to press on with the hard work needed to succeed. And if you're going to implement your dream-job plan, you'll need all the motivation you can get.

TALES OF THE JUMP

Pin Chen was featured on the first season of *Jump Shipp*. With the show's help, Pin thought through her dream and developed a business plan for what is now the Crescendo Young Musicians Guild (cymg.org). The Web site describes the organization as:

> a non-profit music education and community service organization that provides quality music instruction, mentoring, and performance opportunities to students who may otherwise not have them. CYMG promotes a spirit of service while bringing students and families of all cultural and socioeconomic backgrounds together to work toward a common goal: to enrich their communities through music.
>
> CYMG focuses on three main areas:
>
> **Education** – Providing beginning to intermediate music students of all socio-economic backgrounds equal opportunity access to music instruction and giving advanced music students the opportunity to coach younger students under the guidance of professional teaching artists.
>
> **Performance** – Encouraging students to share their music with the public and develop their confidence through performances throughout the year.
>
> **Service** – Serving the community and the organization while growing as members of society through performances and workshops at charity events, in convalescent homes, children's hospitals, and orphanages.

Tell us a bit about your transition.

My life has been centered on music for as long as I can remember. I began singing solos in choir at the age of three and taking violin lessons with my father at the age of six. Piano lessons followed a year after, and by the time I was fourteen, I was teaching private violin lessons myself. It was at that time that I knew I wanted to be a music teacher when I grew up. Everything I've done since then has been to make myself into the best music educator I can be. I received my bachelor of music in music education at Northwestern University and went straight into public school teaching. I am now going into my tenth year of teaching.

Throughout my teaching career so far, I have been laid off multiple times, jumping from district to district, since I've always been low in seniority when school districts were making cuts. When I signed on to do the *Jump Shipp* episode, I had just been laid off by the Los Angeles Unified School District—the fourth school district I had worked for in my then seven years of teaching.

Being laid off so many times and always having to find another job was wearing on me, and it made me think about what I had been dreaming about doing for a long time: starting a music education nonprofit that would serve kids of all different socioeconomic backgrounds. This was never something that I thought I could go and do until I was older and married, but maybe the time for me to accomplish it was *now*. I had taught students in affluent neighborhoods, and I had taught at-risk, disadvantaged students. I had a passion for teaching both, and there wasn't anything out there that specifically brings those different populations together to serve the community through music.

Jump Shipp was just the kick in the butt that I needed to make my dream a reality. No more waiting for the right time— the community needs this!

As you put your dreams into motion, how did your plans change? What surprised you?

After I put my plans into motion to start CYMG, I got a job offer at a high school with a large, prestigious orchestra program. It seemed like a terrific fit for me, so I accepted it. I, therefore, could only work on CYMG in my free time, so it slowed my initial progress by a couple months. So technically, I didn't jump ship. Instead, I just added what I wanted to do onto my plate. Right now it is an appetizer, but perhaps one day it'll become the main course.

As the organization has been growing, I've been surprised at how there's truly a never-ending list of things to do. Every time I think I've checked off everything on my list, there's at least another three things that need to be done.

What kind of setbacks did you face, and how did you go about overcoming them?

There is constantly the issue of the cart before the horse. For instance, in order to get tax-deductible donations, you need to have nonprofit status. In order to get nonprofit status, you should already have some programs running to prove your charity mission. To solve this, I found a fiscal sponsor, and CYMG became a sponsored project, making us eligible to receive tax-deductible donations. We just needed to pay a monthly membership and give them 6 percent of whatever we raise.

Marketing and publicity are just as difficult as fund-raising. For our first workshop, we had a small turnout, even though we offered them completely for free! It was very disappointing, but we just kept going. The workshops gave us a chance to try things out before starting our first school year of classes.

I suppose I've always thought of myself as a realist, but with

CYMG, I have a vision of what this nonprofit can be like, what kind of impact it can make. It's difficult for me to be patient, and every time we do something new, I have high expectations that aren't met. Do I lower my expectations and allow time to grow, to take baby steps? I realized that I do need to be a little more realistic of what we can do right now as a small, young operation but always have the bigger picture in mind to stay motivated.

How did people around you respond to the process? Were you able to find support in your community?

Some of my friends and family were supportive and continue to be actively supportive of the nonprofit—becoming board members, volunteering, and donating. Others, surprisingly, were only superficially supportive. True, my social life greatly diminished as I took on this mission, and thus my personal relationships with many of my friends were stunted. I'm trying to find a better balance so that I can still grow these relationships and grow the nonprofit together.

I have been fortunate to find support from some churches, schools, and businesses that are allowing us to use their space for free to run our classes. I have also been able to find volunteers in and out of the area, (as far as New York and Toronto!) to help with various tasks that I am by no means an expert in, such as graphic design and accounting.

Did you ever consider giving up?

The thought has certainly crossed my mind, especially during the very difficult times when I feel like I am doing 95 percent of the work for the organization, staying up late at night working on CYMG business after coming home from a full day of work for a job I do get paid for. I do think from time to time, "What if this all fails? Maybe that wouldn't be so bad . . . I'd have a life again." I can feel myself on the verge of burning out sometimes, and I really don't want to. But then I think about all those kids that are without the chance to learn music, without something that they can call their own, without something they feel like they can be successful at and express themselves through. I think of all the young people that I can inspire to become educators and better citizens by giving back to society. CYMG's mission is too important to give up. I know I can't do it by myself, so my job is to convince enough people to take the journey with me so that eventually the organization can operate like a real nonprofit corporation, complete with staff and a facility where CYMG students can come to find a safe, welcoming, and creative environment to thrive.

When did you finally feel like you had "arrived"?

I think with each milestone, I feel more and more like I've "arrived." There are two instances where I felt it the most. The first was at our first concert at the end of our first semester, where all the students came together to perform and people in the community got a chance to see firsthand what we were about. I was like a proud mama. CYMG was my baby, and watching those kids perform onstage was like watching my own kids perform (if I had any). The second moment was when I opened the letter from the IRS, determining Crescendo Young Musicians Guild as an official 501(c)(3), about eighteen months after I began the whole process of forming the organization. It was such a long process, but there it was on a piece a paper, stating that CYMG was an official nonprofit!

Step Seven: Mastering and Mentoring

There is a somewhat magical element to the word *mastery*. When I think about a master, I tend to think about those wise old ninja masters we watched in all those kung fu movies growing up. These days, those figures are being reimagined in movies like *Kill Bill* or *Kung Fu Panda*.

What I love about these characters is that, to the average person, it almost seems like they have lost their edge. Sure, they dispense some wisdom, but when it comes to the art itself, are they past their prime?

Not at all. In fact, it's just the opposite. They have become so skilled at their practice, they no longer need to show off. They know when to use it and when it's not needed. And it always seems to be near the end of the movie when the kung fu master is put to the test and displays the skills we secretly knew he had in him all along.

We learn similar lessons along the way to our dream job. There is an old saying that the older we get, the more we know how much we don't actually know. I feel this is true in my own life, and my mentors have shared similar feelings with me as well. This is when we realize that the editing of our dream job, the story we are telling with our life, never actually stops. You never fully "arrive" at the end. It is a continual process that we, over time, get better at understanding. By editing your plan, you realize that, even as you advance into your thirties and forties and beyond, you have the capacity to take risks, to fail and succeed. When we give up our willingness to take a risk, we give up that part of ourselves that was created to search for more—not necessarily another dollar, but another achievement, another contribution to society.

As you continue to edit and define your dream job, you also realize through your success that there are many other people who, whether you've noticed them or not, are following in your footsteps. They are in the e-mails in your in-box, asking you questions. They want to know how you dealt with issues they are now dealing with. They want to know how you got to where you are—*your* "origin story."

This is an important "full circle" moment in your life that is important to pay attention to and respect. Those who come behind you are seeking out their path, searching to make a name for themselves, just as you once sought out guides and mentors. Each of them has a unique Y factor that got them to you, and each of them has a specific Z factor they are pursuing. In the meantime, they are figuring out how to deal with where they are in their X factor, and you have the opportunity to help them.

By becoming a master and offering your expertise, you are completing the circle you started at the beginning of this process. George Leonard, an American writer famous for his work in education and human potential, knew a thing or two about mastery. He even wrote the book on it, called *Mastery,* when he was in his late sixties.

He didn't just pull this stuff out of thin air. Leonard was once a bomber pilot and instructor in the U.S. Army Air Corp, achieved remarkable status as a prolific and gifted author and teacher, served as president of several organizations and associations, and, to my endless amazement, held a fifth-degree black belt in aikido, a highly disciplined Japanese martial art that uses the attacker's force and momentum against them. (He didn't even start training until he was forty-seven years old and continued to practice and teach into his eighties!)

According to Leonard, "mastery" encompasses a lot of elements. Here are just a few of his points that I found extremely helpful:

- Long-term dedication to the journey—not the bottom line
- Knowing that you will never reach a final destination
- Being willing to practice, even when you seem to be getting nowhere
- Being fully in the present moment
- Being willing to look foolish
- Maintaining flexibility in your strategy and actions

We tend to assume that mastery is out of reach—something only available to those born with exceptional abilities and natural talent and to little green aliens with giant ears who speak in broken sentences and live to be nine hundred years old. But, the truth is, you can—and indeed will—become a master. Mastery isn't reserved for the extremely talented or those fortunate enough to have gotten an early start. It is available to anyone who is willing to get on the path and stay on it, and it doesn't matter how old you are or what you've done in the past. It is a lifelong pursuit.

DO THIS STEP OR ELSE

Obviously, if you have taken the following six steps and are continuing to move forward into step seven, you have set yourself apart from the pack. You have established yourself as a worker, someone in the top percentile. You are motivated. Prepared. Your dream is not made of fluff and you are not leaning back on grandiose ideas. You have brought something into existence, and hopefully you are reaping the benefits of it.

Can I be blunt?

As a master, you have the right to become a total jerk. It's true. You put in the work. You put in the hours. You stayed up late at night. You have created something no one else had the vision or the knowledge to create. It was your blood, sweat, and tears. And you know what? I applaud you because you are awesome. That is what this book was all about—making you awesome at your dream job. And you've done it. So the next move is up to you. You have the option to accept all of the praise that the world is giving you, buy a home in the Hamptons, and chill by your awesome backyard pool sipping piña coladas.

Or you can choose to use your mastery to start to give back through mentoring. The choice is up to you.

Call it karma. Call it love. Call it leadership. Call it what you want. But I believe that those who have been given much are also responsible for giving much in return. And you, my friend, as a newfound master, have been given much. So don't sit back and become that jerk who laughs at those trying to follow in your footsteps. You are in a position to become the type of leader who brings his followers along and encourages them to surpass his own greatness. Be the type of leader who will use your talents to give others a helping hand.

In the creation of this book, I'm using the small amount of

mastery I've achieved and offering it back to you. So please, consider following my advice: advise, mentor, give back.

WHY YOU'LL SETTLE

Achieving success has the potential to make you lazy. Why? Because you have already established yourself as being good enough. But you won't master your dream if you give into the lie of "good enough." Yes, you're good enough to pay your bills. You're good enough to spend several more weeks on vacation each year. Maybe you're good enough to speak at a TED conference. So why keep trying to improve?

Because even when you think you've peaked, you're still learning. You're programming your brain or body for new challenges. You're making conscious processes subconscious. Second nature. You're literally training yourself—even when you think you've reached the crest. And if you don't have a chance to catch your breath and internalize what you experienced on the climb, you'll never be ready to make the next one.

Picture it as the "Saving" progress bar in computer software. I have several friends who are graphic designers and work all day in Adobe Photoshop creating massive files. When they click "Save," it doesn't happen instantly. The program locks down for a bit while the file saves. Nothing happens. Yet something very important is happening all the while. Then, all of a sudden, it's done. The long process of saving, when seemingly nothing was happening, has resulted in a measurable achievement: The file is saved. The knowledge that you have achieved a success is now yours to hold on to, to use as an authoritative example of what happens when you strive for greatness.

Maybe you've heard the saying, "It's lonely at the top." Well, it's true. Many of today's most successful people have done everything necessary to put them on the top of the dog pile, only to eventually realize that there isn't a lot of room for friends. Oftentimes, they are looking for others to reach out to them. Maybe you feel similarly. So don't be shy about making yourself available, looking for new resources, collaborators, accountability partners.

SHAKE IT UP

As an expert, you will find numerous opportunities to teach others, but it is extremely important for you to continue to develop yourself. Many established professionals have put in their time before the settling bug finally creeps up on them and whispers in their ear that they don't need to search anymore, that they've done enough, that they've reached the summit and now they can rest on their laurels.

The truth is that there is nothing sadder than seeing someone settle for a plateau along the journey, all the while believing they've reached the peak. There's always a higher summit, always another revision of the dream to make. And one of those summits involves passing along what you've learned, passing along your legacy.

POSSIBLE HURDLES

Again, this is a *nice problem to have,* but because of the incredible job you have displayed overcoming the previous six steps, you're in a position to give back. Now, before we get all congratulatory, there's one thing you need to know. The potential hurdles you will inevitably face in step seven are all based in pride. Pride leads us to the laziness that comes from thinking you are all that, the best, at the top of your game. Sure, you will have those moments, but you must realize that your dream job is bigger than you. It also involves the well-being of your family as well as the future of your employees, your users, and your clients. All of these people are relying on your mastery to serve them in some way or another. These people have become your responsibility. You need to take care of them.

Avoid the laziness by continuing to push forward, continually creating your list of your three actions to accomplish. Even when you feel you've made it to the top, don't stop. You never know what is possible.

I could have easily made a career speaking to teen audiences, but I knew there was so much more that I could be a part of. Instead of relaxing into a familiar routine of speaking, I have had the chance to create two television shows and two books, and I'm developing a company to expand my leadership, helping mentor and guide other speakers who are following behind me. I want to use what little mastery I've achieved to branch out. I want to find new industries to master and eager new people to mentor.

This brings me to the next potential hurdle you must face. You need to avoid investing your wisdom in people who—how shall I say—don't deserve it. I don't mean to be harsh, but it's often that we spend time talking with people who don't have the guts to make their dreams come true. As I said earlier, I have my own gut feeling when I talk with someone and you will also develop your own spidey-sense to understand who has what it takes to make their dreams happen—and who doesn't. In the words of Steven Pressfield, "a gunslinger always recognizes another gunslinger." When they show up, even if they haven't reached the same level of mastery, you'll recognize the potential in someone. When you see them, make yourself available to them and invest in their future. If they don't seem to strike that magical harmonic chord in you, be polite and save your time for that hidden gem. Invest your time as a mentor wisely in people who truly have the capacity to do something extraordinary with it.

MAKING THE JUMP

So here we are. You've made it through the six previous steps. You wrote down your dream and refined it. You did your research and even kicked the tires a bit on your dream. You decided the best path to take. You identified the first three action steps to take—and knocked them out (and did it over and over again). You've made the jump.

Along the path to seeing your dream become a reality, you've learned a lot—how to deal with failure, setbacks, and plateaus. You've climbed and climbed and climbed. But here's the thing:

You're not finished. Not by a long shot.

You see, once you've seen a dream become reality, the feeling can become intoxicating. Trust me, I know. Once you see one dream come true, you want to see another one, and another. With the success you've achieved, allow newer and even crazier dreams into your brain. See if you can take them through the Josh Shipp Patented Seven-Step Blueprint for Dream-Job Fulfillment. I dare you. The bottom line is this: Once you've attained your dream, don't think you've arrived. There are other dreams to be realized.

People on the leading edge are always learners. Think back to the people you sought out as interviewees and mentors in step three. I bet that if you look at what they have in common, one thing will jump out at you—they were are all constantly striving to know more and do better. They sought not just to succeed in their dream, but also to exceed their expectations. If you want to master your craft, it's not just about climbing to the summit and planting your flag in the ground. It's about pushing the limits of what's possible. It's about never settling. Maybe it's researching your craft more deeply. Maybe it's continually seeking out the expertise of others in the field. Perhaps it's finding a way to gain even greater experience. Whatever it is, to master your craft it is critical that you position yourself as a learner, first and foremost. Because when the thrill of achieving your dream starts to fade a bit—and it will—it's that struggle to know more and do better that will keep you going.

And again, stay open to helping others. Think of it as a way to leave a legacy. Think of it as a way to pay back those who poured their time, effort, and expertise into you when you were still flailing around with your dream. Think of it however you want. Choose to live your life as an example—as a reservoir of experience. Be willing to give your time, your talent, your expertise, and your money. In doing so, you'll be honoring those who helped you become what you are, as well as those who are following in your footsteps.

And isn't that what it's really all about anyway? It's not just about living a comfortable life (whatever that means). Anyone can do that. It's not even about seeing your dream become a reality. It's about living that unlived life. Fulfilling your calling. It's about being able to leave a mark on society, to leave a legacy worth the effort and energy you put into it—the long hours, the late nights, the emotional cost. It's about inspiring others to dream crazy dreams—and seeing them actually make it.

Yeah, that's something worth jumping for.

TALES OF THE JUMP

Chris Evans has cofounded three tech companies, the first when he was eighteen years old and a freshman in college. All three were successful, and the third, Accipiter, helped define the business of Internet advertising. After a larger company acquired it, Chris elected to spend more time with his family and in helping nonprofit organizations get off the ground. With his children reaching college age, he's recently refocused on for-profit ventures.

How has your dream job been different from what you expected?

Most of all, it's because it's three different dream jobs at present. I'm publishing a book, mentoring a first-time entrepreneur with a very exciting new technology, and teaching a thought-provoking class on topics that range from ghost hunting to the effects of minimum wage income to the challenge of teens making themselves vulnerable to each other. They are all very different contexts and it keeps me thinking creatively all the time.

So would you say working on different, seemingly disconnected projects, can help inspire your central goals?

Yes, in the sense that the ideas and people that turn up in one project can often carry over to others. But this isn't a strategy I'd recommend to most people. It's very hard to divide your time and focus between several goals and not have all of them suffer. Earlier in my career, I was much more single-minded in my pursuits, and I think it was the momentum from my success then that makes it possible to do things the way I do now.

What are your dreams now? How have you continued to grow within your dream job?

Any time I take on a project or venture, I always like to know where it might go if it gets really big overnight. I know the next several products I would build on top of my book, who might acquire my entrepreneur's start-up, and how I would syndicate the class I teach to other schools. Then I dig down to what needs to happen right this month—what's the task at hand. You can't get so wrapped up in the long-term dream that you don't take care of business now, but you need to be working toward a big idea. One last thing, it's fine (and probably likely) that my ventures could take a totally unexpected turn if they take off. The point of having the vision isn't to force your actions into that mold. It's to make sure you at least know one way you can succeed that you really believe in.

The other way I grow is through personal development. As someone who believes in God, I seek out his guidance regularly. I'm also constantly on the lookout for opportunities that might arise because I believe he's guiding me. It's almost like a treasure hunt. I never know who I'll meet that will change my life, or what article or book I'll read that will offer the solution to a big problem, but I've come to trust that a higher power is behind the scenes setting these things up. I stay on the lookout for them.

Do you have a secret for contentment?

For me, this also goes to my faith. The thing I'm most invested in isn't success or the next big thing or money. It's in the bigger picture. For me, that's God, but for some it might be family or other ideologies. If I don't let my identity as an author, as an entrepreneur, or as a teacher be the center of my life, then I don't stress out when I experience setbacks in those areas. Sure, I want to succeed, but I can truly embrace the times when things don't work out right as an opportunity to learn and reaffirm where my heart really is.

How have you been able to give back or help others following in your footsteps?

I have met with dozens of entrepreneurs and teams to give them feedback on their plans and ideas and to help them see new opportunities and strategies for their ventures. Something I try to do is to give them honest feedback and let them know when their plan isn't good enough yet or when they've overlooked an important area. This feedback is critical. Everyone likes to root for an entrepreneur, and it's always tempting just to jump on board and tell them you believe in their vision; but entrepreneurship is

also very tough, and they need to know the challenges they're
facing and truly have weighed the cost when they get started so
they don't lose heart later.

**What do you think is the single most valuable trait in making an
entrepreneurial endeavor work?**
Entrepreneurs succeed by managing trust. When you're starting
with nothing, the first resource you can get access to is trust. If
you accumulate enough of it, you can use it to gain other resources,
like investments, employees, customers, press exposure, and stra-
tegic partners. A keen understanding of when people trust and
why they don't allows entrepreneurs to figure out how to solve
the problems ahead of them.

To answer your next question: Trust is gained through a
combination of a focus, a detailed vision of your venture, and
personal integrity.

Final Words . . .

And so our journey has come to an end. And even though we may be parting ways in this book, there's something I really want you to know.

You have done something truly remarkable. Seriously.

Maybe you don't feel like it right now, but just think about it. You've gone from realizing you're stuck to actually doing something about it. A depressing number of people come to this realization and then do nothing because of fear, the cost, or the unknown. Many people start this journey only to bail somewhere along the way or wind up shipwrecked off some uncharted desert isle.

Well, maybe them. **But not YOU.**

You've decided to pursue something better. You've set your sights on something bigger. You've decided to put in the hard work, the dedication, the commitment in order to pursue your dream—something you were made to do, something that has a lasting impact, not only on you but also on those who are following in your footsteps. You've decided to leave a mark.

So there's something I really want you to know. If you've

made it this far, you have separated yourself from the pack. You
are a pioneer—a trailblazer.

Pioneers lead the way. They take great risks. They push forward despite all obstacles. They overcome. They refuse to stop.
They are the ones who discover new territory. They go where no
one has gone before. (Sound familiar?)

They look to the horizon and are not limited by what they
know or have been told by others. They break the mold. Constructs and ways of thinking and acting that circumscribe others
do not define them. They take the best from their context but do
not let it limit them. They dream big dreams but then they invest themselves fully to bring that dream to reality. They break
molds, they smash barriers, they shatter preconceptions, and they
push through resistance at all levels to achieve their goals. They
are willing to pay any price, make any sacrifice, and fight any foe
to reach their dream.

A pioneer. That's you.

Along the way you've allowed yourself to dream. You've written the dream down in black and white. You've refined the
dream by doing the hard work or researching what it *really* takes
to see your dream become a reality. Maybe you had to do this a
few (dozen) times to make sure that what you wanted was really
what you wanted. No matter, you charged forward anyway—
blazing a new trail.

You took your dream for a test-drive. You kicked the tires.
Slid in behind the wheel. Smelled the interior. You found out
what it really takes to live the dream you want. (And you also
probably met a few interesting people along the way.) You decided what would be the best path to take and began creating a
unique plan—three action steps at a time.

And then you jumped!

Three steps after three steps after three steps—and before you knew it, you were doing what you had only dreamed of in the beginning. You were seeing your dream become a reality. You were living it.

Most people come to a book like this looking for certain kinds of answers. They're looking for the "overnight solution" or the "ten foolproof, can't-fail ideas for securing everything you ever wanted in life and more. . . ."

Think for a second about the difference between a trail map and a compass.

Most people come to a book like this looking for a well-defined path. Start here. Do this. Then do that. Say this. Go after that. Follow this trail, and, in the end, somehow magically, you'll wind up in the right destination. But I have news for you: Life just doesn't work like that. And anyone who tries to sell you on some fail-proof "formula for success" is just a huckster.

Now, I can understand why people are drawn to this kind of thing. People want to be told what to do. They want to be given a specific path, their steps outlined with precision. They want check boxes and lists. Something to measure themselves by. They want assurances.

But not you.

My hope in writing this book was simple. I didn't want to blow smoke at you, giving you some lame list of things to do.

Rather than giving you a trail map, I wanted to give you a compass.

You see, a compass is about finding your unique direction. It's about taking you from where you are to where you want to be. A compass can be used at any point along the journey—even if for some reason you get off the path and find yourself lost in the woods. It can always help you get back on the right path and show you the right direction. But the walking is up to you. The hard work of heading in the right direction is up to you.

The seven steps are not some magical incantation for getting your dream job. They are about setting you in the right direction and helping you discover the right steps. They are about giving you the tools to forge ahead. They are not a formula, not a map. The seven steps are a compass to help direct you on your own path.

But in the end, it's really up to you.

You are the only one that can make your dream happen. No one is going to stop you on the street and offer you your dream job. (Well, I guess if you're Gisele Bündchen they might.) Are you willing to do the necessary work, research, planning, and preparation needed to see your dream make it into a reality? If you've made it this far in the book—the answer is pretty clear.

You are.

You see, this is your dream. You discovered it. You refined it. You planned and prepared for it. You've done the hard work necessary. You've invested your time, effort, and energy—and so have others. This is not merely a dream—it's becoming a reality. The path is set. You know what you need to do. And now it's time.

You got your pants on?

FTL drive is spooled up.

Boards are green.

3 . . . 2 . . . 1 . . .

Jump.

APPENDIX

Worksheets and Additional Resources

PERSONALITY TESTS

As you can probably tell from having read this book, I feel that a lot of the bigger personal issues we face are because we don't know ourselves. We may see ourselves as victims of our past. Or maybe we're too scared to make a decision in the present or to venture forward out of our comfort zones. A lot of these issues lie deep within our personalities and are based on personal experience and life-changing moments. So sometimes it's good to be open to figuring out who we really are so we can start to change our behaviors and make better decisions for the future.

Before I go on, I want you to know there is no shame in seeking help from a counselor. I've been there and pretty much all the smart people I've ever come across have seen counselors in order to deal with their issues. Now, if you aren't ready for that, that's fine; I would like to suggest that you take a few small steps that can help you do some self-discovery. I've taken all the personality tests listed below, and it's amazing to see how they all line up.

Like I've said before: You need to be open and do the hard work—to ask yourself the tough questions, to write a journal, and, when you're ready, to ask your friends and mentors to be completely honest with you about the ways in which you can improve. This can be a great step forward as you start to explore the motivations behind your actions. In the meantime, these tools can be a great step forward as you start to explore the motivations behind your actions.

Enneagram Personality Test (http://www.enneagraminstitute .com). This is an ancient and fascinating way to look at personality types. According to the Enneagram, there are only nine personality types. This test has been one of the most influential tools I've used to assist in making decisions and in measuring if they are coming from a healthy or unhealthy place. It's a little geeky because it's so intense, but when you start to wrap your head around it, you'll discover a whole new filter through which to see the world. You'll find reasons to offer extended amounts of grace to yourself and others in your life since you can see they are making decisions based out of the unhealthy portions of their personality type.

Myers-Briggs Type Indicator (http://www.myersbriggs.org/). This test is a corporate go-to, an old standby. Many people speak in the Myers-Briggs language, and the test can become the catalyst to many future conversations about why people make the decisions they make. The Myers-Briggs test is based in Jungian psychology and bases its determination of how you view the world on four constructs: Extroverted versus Introverted, Sensing versus Intuition, Thinking versus Feeling, and Judging versus Perceiving.

StrengthsFinder Resource and Materials (http://www.strengths finder.com). I really like this approach, which is based on the work of Donald O. Clifton and the Gallup organization's research methodology. StrengthsFinder has concluded that each of us have access to thirty-four different strengths. Naturally, however, we tend to lean toward our top five to ten strengths. The basic premise of becoming a "well-rounded person" is a bunch of crap. Authors like Marcus Buckingham and Tom Rath have written books that help show you how to locate and increase your strengths while letting go of your weaknesses.

This is a very freeing exercise since it helps you quit beating yourself up over why you love the big picture and hate details (or vice versa).

HELPFUL SITES

TED (http://www.ted.com). Video collection of new innovative thinkers. Constant inspiration!

99 U (http://99u.com/). Insights on making ideas happen.

Kickstarter (http://www.kickstarter.com). Kickstarter is a funding platform for creative projects.

Dream Year (http://www.dreamyear.net). Coaching Web site for solidifying and creating your dream job in one full year.

Start Garden (http://www.startgarden.com). Investment company that supports two new ideas each week. The first is chosen by the company, and the second is voted on by the public.

Startup America Partnership (http://www.s.co/). A growing partnership network to invest in young businesses.

Springwise (http://www.springwise.com). Sharing new business ideas for entrepreneurs.

MySubplot (http://www.mysubplot.com). Helping you live a better story using timeless storytelling principles. MySubplot has a spiritual approach but is applicable to everyone.

HELPFUL BOOKS

Art and Fear: Observations on the Perils (and Rewards) of Artmaking, by David Bayles and Ted Orland

Blue Ocean Strategy: How to Create Uncontested Market

Space and Make Competition Irrelevant, by W. Chan Kim
and Renée Mauborgne

*The Brand Called You: The Ultimate Brand-Building and
Business Development Handbook to Transform Anyone
into an Indispensable Personal Brand,* by Peter Montoya
with Tim Vandehey

Crush It!: Why Now Is the Time to Cash In on Your Passion,
by Gary Vaynerchuk

The Dip: A Little Book That Teaches You When to Quit, by
Seth Godin

Do the Work, by Steven Pressfield

*The E-Myth Revisited: Why Most Small Businesses Don't
Work and What to Do About It,* by Michael E. Gerber

*The Four-Hour Workweek: Escape 9–5, Live Anywhere, and
Join the New Rich,* by Timothy Ferriss

Getting Things Done: The Art of Stress-Free Productivity, by
David Allen

*Good to Great: Why Some Companies Make the Leap . . . and
Others Don't,* by Jim Collins

*The Lean Startup: How Today's Entrepreneurs Use Continu-
ous Innovation to Create Radically Successful Businesses,*
by Eric Ries

*Making Ideas Happen: Overcoming the Obstacles Between
Vision and Reality,* by Scott Belsky

*The $100 Startup: Reinvent the Way You Make a Living,
Do What You Love, and Create a New Future,* by Chris
Guillebeau

Platform: Get Noticed in a Noisy World, by Michael Hyatt

*Quitter: Closing the Gap Between Your Day Job and Your
Dream Job,* by Jon Acuff

*Rules of the Red Rubber Ball: Find and Sustain Your Life's
Work,* by Kevin Carroll

Storyline: Finding Your Subplot in God's Story, by Donald Miller

Strengthfinder 2.0, by Tom Rath

The Total Money Makeover: A Proven Plan for Financial Fitness, by David Ramsey

The Truth About You: Your Secret to Success, by Marcus Buckingham

The War of Art: Break Through the Blocks and Win Your Inner Creative Battles, by Steven Pressfield

The Wisdom of the Enneagram: The Complete Guide to Psychological and Spiritual Growth for The Nine Personality Types, by Don Richard Riso and Russ Hudson

ACKNOWLEDGMENTS

Dearest Reader,

The following is a list of smart / attractive / glorious / caring / supportive people you probably don't know along with a list of inside jokes you won't get.

I apologize in advance.

Sarah Shipp: I love you.

London Shipp: You're a good man, Charlie Brown.

Katherine Shipp: Thank you, baby Katie.

Rodney and Christine Weidenmaier: Thanks for seeing what I couldn't see.

Alex and Roxanne Petruncola: I love being a part of your family.

Gary Jones: Mentors change people. You are proof.

Kathy McRice: I miss you. You taught us all how to love.

Jeffrey Van Wootton: Griffey.

Tuesday Night, Inc: Iron sharpens Iron.

The 5am Running Squad: I deeply appreciate the miles and friendship. YES, even you Eric.

Sir Marc Davis: FWI—you are freaking awesome.

Brooks Gibbs: Thanks for being a great wingman.

Jason Marshall: Can you speak up?

Ezra Gordon: Love you like a brother.

Erin Niumata: Thanks for your constant support and professionalism.

David Wenzel: You may be a three with a four wing. But this book is a ten.

Michael Colletto and Jordan Green: Two for two. You guys are diamonds in the rough.

Mike DeVries: You really are "the Wolf."

Kirk Flatow: This book is only 95 percent your material.

Chase Reeves: Insert animated .gif here.

Isaiah Torres: I am so deeply proud of you. Even if you ARE taller than me.

Jon Talbert: Your care for the less fortunate is remarkable.

Dr. Samuel Talbert: Hello, Mr. Chip.

Westgate: It's an honor to be a part of your family.

Erin Garay: Your turn.

Rick Lu: Thank you for your wisdom.

Bryn Freedman: Where IS Sharon?

Team TT: Barb, AV, and Ron—Push In.

St. Martins: Thanks for your commitment to excellence and for pushing us to give the best.

Jamie Oliver: You smash my perception of realistic and Italian food.

Halogen: You are the change. It's a true delight to partner with you guys.

Ken and Aimee VanMeter: Love you both dearly and your salsa.

Max Stubblefield: Hey Buddy, thanks for blowing things up.

Ellen Rakieten: Thanks for taking a chance on this kid.

Dr. Joe Martin: I challenge you to a p90x dual.

Fabian Ramirez: Can't wait to see where you take things.

David Edward Garcia: Thanksgiving Blend for life!

Kantis Simmons: Remember what you said to the reporter?

Brandon Spinazzola: You are brilliant.

Jeff Slobotski: Quick fingers lead to book acknowledgment.

And to Ben Arment, Pin Chen, Abbie Cobb, Heather Colletto, Ryan Duffy, Chris Evans, Sue Fletcher, Mindy Green, Jonathan Stoner, Caton Vance, and Erik Wahl—thanks for letting us tell your stories!

ABOUT JOSH SHIPP

Josh Shipp stars in the documentary TV series *Teen Trouble* and *Jump Shipp*. He's the founder of Youth Speaker University and was listed in *Inc.* magazine's 30 Under 30 list of successful entrepreneurs. He has spoken at Harvard, Stanford, UCLA, MIT, and to over two million young adults live. He has contributed as a behavioral expert for such outlets as MTV, CNN, *Anderson Live, Good Morning America, The New York Times,* Oprah.com, and more.

Abandoned and abused as a child and raised in many different foster homes, Josh has taken his past of hurt and neglect, and turned it around, using it as a catalyst for helping others.

Say hello at www.JoshShipp.com.